# BECOMING
# COACH JAKE

*A Story of Overcoming the Odds,
on the Soccer Field and Beyond*

## MARTIN JACOBSON
### WITH BILL SAPORITO

Foreword by Don Garber
Afterword by Kyle Martino

Skyhorse Publishing

Skyhorse Publishing books may be purchased in bulk at special discounts for sales promotion, corporate gifts, fund-raising, or educational purposes. Special editions can also be created to specifications. For details, contact the Special Sales Department, Skyhorse Publishing, 307 West 36th Street, 11th Floor, New York, NY 10018 or info@skyhorsepublishing.com.

Skyhorse® and Skyhorse Publishing® are registered trademarks of Skyhorse Publishing, Inc.®, a Delaware corporation.

Visit our website at www.skyhorsepublishing.com.

10 9 8 7 6 5 4 3 2 1

Library of Congress Cataloging-in-Publication Data is available on file.

Cover design by Tom Lau
Cover photograph courtesy of Martin Jacobson

ISBN: 978-1-5107-4222-2
Ebook ISBN 978-1-5107-4223-9

Printed in the United States of America

# Contents

# Foreword

By Don Garber
Commissioner, Major League Soccer

THE STORY OF MARTIN JACOBSON—OR "Coach Jake," as everyone knows him—truly mirrors the story of soccer in the United States.

Like the rise of our sport in this country, Coach Jake's tale is about embracing the role of the underdog, taking on challenges, and answering the skeptics. Thanks to the passionate fans, talented players, and entrepreneurs who believe in our league and this great game, Major League Soccer has grown significantly in North America during the last twenty-five years. The extraordinary success of Jake and his teams occurred during the same time frame.

On his path to success as a coach, guidance counselor, and athletic director at Martin Luther King, Jr. High School in New York, Jake overcame significant adversity in the form of drug addiction. But while reading this book, keep in mind that Jake would be the first to tell you that his story is not just about him. Among many other things, it is a testament to the incredible young men that have filled his rosters and won 18 New York City PSAL championships in his tenure. For many of them, soccer was the path to their American dreams.

Jake's teams have been a reflection of the extraordinary diversity of our country and game. Especially during this time of intense debate over immigration in our country, the story of *Becoming Coach Jake* is enlightening and should never be forgotten. In the end, it was the game of soccer, his players, staff, and family that saved him.

Soccer teaches us many invaluable and inspiring lessons. I hope you will take from Jake's book the powerful messages he shares from three decades as a leader, educator, and coach.

# Prologue

Soccer is called the beautiful game but for me, the game is beyond beautiful. Soccer is my savior, a game that offered personal redemption from a life nearly red-carded by drug addiction.

How could I thank this game for giving me life? I'm going to tell you. For the last two decades, I have been the soccer coach at Martin Luther King, Jr. High School on New York City's West Side. Our school had a bad reputation. Our soccer team had no reputation. We didn't even have a home field. We still don't. Yet our kids won New York City's high school soccer championship 18 times during that period, most recently the 2018 season when we went undefeated and untied.

More importantly, we win in the classroom, too. Our team has a graduation rate of 96 percent in a city that struggles to get to 70 percent. And did I mention that many of the kids I coach are immigrants, who often arrive here facing more challenges than a one-armed goalkeeper?

This is not a particularly good time to be the coach of a high school soccer team whose driving force is immigrants. Here in New York, a metropolis created and shaped by immigrants and their descendants, the hurdles have never been higher for teens from "shithole countries," as our nativist president described them, who want to graduate high school and move on to bigger opportunities. But as the Lady in New

York Harbor says, *Send these, the homeless, tempest-tossed to me, I lift my lamp beside the golden door!*

I am a lamp lifter, like the Lady, not someone trying to slam the golden door shut. I have shown hundreds of immigrant kids—some of them parentless, some of them hungry and homeless, all of them struggling to find a place in this teeming city—that the promise of our nation is very much alive. They can arrive from nowhere. One day a couple of years ago I got a call from a woman from Cote d'Ivoire who told me she was sheltering four kids who arrived here legally but had been abandoned by their supposed sponsors. They were facing deportation. I was able to get all of these boys enrolled at MLK. These high schoolers are good kids, great students, and they have soccer talent that helped MLK win the 2017 and 2018 championships. They have tons of promise as future US citizens whether they go on to play professional soccer or not.

I know this story on a personal level, too. Mansour Ndiaye was once one of those kinds of kids. He appeared in my office in 1996, taken there by a relative, poorly dressed in ill-fitting clothing that belied the elegance of his soccer skills. He was looking for a place to play, to learn. He never seemed to be far away from me—or a book—always craving direction, coaching, and okay, a meal. So my wife Connie and I raised him as our own, beginning in 1997. Today, Mansour Ndiaye, Ph.D., is a member of the faculty at the University of Connecticut.

Not all of our kids become this successful—no educator can make that claim. We all "lose" kids who take the wrong path or get bad advice along the way. But it saddens me that the promise once offered to these children seems to be imperiled by an administration and an attitude that has recast immigrants as people who should be targeted for removal rather than encouraged to bring their hopes and talents here.

My own love for soccer is a product of one of those amazing immigrants. He was a German Jew who fled Nazi murderers and, after years of trying, finally arrived in my neighborhood in Long Beach,

New York. He would not be alone among Holocaust survivors in my town, but he would be singular in the gift he would bring to one local kid struggling to find himself as his own father grappled with chronic illness.

Soccer, like much of our nation's sporting heritage, hails from foreign shores. Soccer was, and remains, a game of immigrants. Stop at any field—heck, any open space big enough to set up improvised goals—in New York City or Chicago or Washington D.C. or Los Angeles and you will always see groups of people playing soccer. That's been true for a hundred years. But this immigrants' game has now become America's game—more Texans play soccer than American football. Soccer has become as much a part of our culture as baseball and barbeques. Major League Soccer, our pro league, has never been in better shape, and continues to add franchises and fans.

Soccer, like so many immigrants, is flourishing in America.

So, too, is another import. Heroin. And a more recent arrival, fentanyl. There is a tragic irony evolving in our country. While a growing part of the population is obsessed with fitness and healthy living, the underbelly of drug addiction is growing at horrific rates. In the last three years or so, heroin overdoses have ravaged suburbs like the one I grew up in, as well as rural communities from Georgia to New Hampshire. It's been called an epidemic, although some critics have pointed out that it's an epidemic only because so many working- and middle-class white people have become victims.

The sociopolitical aspects aside, the numbers are staggering. More than seventy thousand people died of overdoses in 2017 according to the National Center for Health Statistics at the Centers for Disease Control and Prevention. That's more than traffic deaths and deaths from guns combined. More than twenty million Americans are addicted to drugs.

So I guess you can call me a trendsetter, a pioneer. I started abusing drugs fifty years ago, long before it was fashionable. I graduated from Ball State University in Indiana in 1968, in the middle of the Midwest, and then earned a master's degree 1971. But deep in America's heartland I learned to like drugs. And when I moved to a city near Detroit, I not only liked drugs, I sold them, all the while holding a day job as a high school teacher, coach, and counselor. It was a façade that took no small amount of perseverance—that trait has an ugly side—and I was able to maintain this conflicting existence of teacher-mentor-coach-druggie for the next three years. My then wife and I would eventually move to Santa Fe, New Mexico, where the charade, along with my life and career, would begin to unravel in the hell of hardcore addiction.

The journey back would include some false starts, a run-in with a potentially fatal disease, and a stopover in a jail that, for all the reasons you would imagine, was called the Tombs. If you are looking for an all-American story with a spotless hero, better go to the fiction section. This isn't *Hoosiers*. This is about a drug-scarred man barely hanging on until soccer, and some immigrant kids who play it, restored his life and his life's work.

# CHAPTER 1
# Eighteen and Counting

THE 40-YARD PASS WAS A feather of a ball and seemed nearly impossible on a raw November day with a brutal 35 mph wind. But there it was, 57 minutes into the game between Martin Luther King, Jr. High School and Curtis High School for the Public Schools Athletic League A championship. We had pounded away at the Curtis defense for the entire first half, but their squad had been unyielding. They were going to defend with all eleven players behind the ball if necessary. In soccer, it's known as "parking the bus."

I had confidence in our players from the very beginning of the season. We knew this was going to be one of our best teams ever, though in a playoff you have to be careful, as all it takes is one bad pass, one lucky shot, and it can all go south.

My nervousness, as usual, was increasing until David Gomez, our slinky central midfielder, spotted Gaoussou Coulibaly just outside the opposing penalty area. Gaoussou cushioned the pass on his right foot almost nonchalantly, turned toward goal, cut inside his marker, and unleashed a vicious shot. Goal. I knew instantly that we were on our way to the 2018 PSAL championship.

Over the next twenty minutes Gaoussou would go on to score a hat trick, and we got another goal from Akeem Shelton, our sensational all-star senior striker, to win 4–0. We would finish the year undefeated, untied, and ranked third nationally on the Top Drawer Soccer poll, a ranking I would gladly put on the line if either of those top two schools would have been willing to play us. It was truly a magical season for the team, or maybe an extension of the last two seasons. In fact, MLK has been on an astonishing three-year streak—59 games without a defeat or even a draw.

That's a pretty good run, and you could say that I've been on an even better run. Since 1994, I've been the head coach of boys soccer at MLK, the most successful high school team in New York City, if not the country. We've won 18 New York City championships in an environment that has sometimes been challenging, sometimes dangerous, sometimes ugly. During that time, MLK became famous first for being infamous—a school branded as Horror High in the tabloids. And I would be the target of a vicious, racist, and ultimately discredited attempt to derail our program. You see, many of our kids are immigrants, or sons of immigrants. Even in New York, historically a city of immigrants, there are always pockets of xenophobia.

But I've learned to play the game: I am more than a coach. I am a guidance counselor and gym teacher by training, but by now more than well versed in immigration law, social work, politics, and media. Whatever it takes to give my kids the best opportunity they can have to become good players and great citizens. Take Gaoussou, a wonderful kid from Cote D'Ivoire who is loved by his teammates for his leadership and work ethic. I have no doubt he will have a successful career, whether it's in soccer or some other occupation. He's got what we call King Heart: a spirit of caring, of taking the responsibility, of being a good teammate.

At our championship celebration in the glamorous MLK cafeteria in early January 2019, there were thirty-seven trophies to be handed out. But I knew that not all the boys would be on hand to collect the honor that they had played so hard to claim. Because some of them were working. They deliver pizzas, sling hamburgers in fast food joints, work as street vendors or in bodegas. And they are not merely trying to get a little spending money together. They are working to survive and help their families survive. That was the case at our first championship and every one since. I have to laugh sometimes when we get criticized for running a "professional" program. How many pros do you know who are busboys on the side?

Let me tell you about three of our team members, some of the best on the squad, who were all abandoned in this country by an unscrupulous sports agent. They were born in Cote D'Ivoire, a once fairly prosperous nation that has been wracked by internecine violence, repression of civil rights, and the ebola epidemic, among other problems.

Of course, having kids on the team who are immigrants has come with its own set of challenges that go way beyond soccer. In one instance years ago, a student got whisked off the streets while he was traveling on a college visit—a traumatic experience, to say the least. In fact, I know personally what it's like to be hauled off the streets and thrown into a federal lockup; I know the incredible chaos and fear that takes place all too well.

The solution, of course, is to work hard to get green cards for those that need them. One of my former players, Jethro Dede, who also hails from Cote D'Ivoire, became a productive US citizen thanks to our efforts. Dede was an All American in high school who went on to graduate from St. Lawrence University. That's how America is supposed to work.

Though we'd never rush a student into college if he wasn't ready, we are always looking for ways to get our kids a college education so they can earn more and be more productive as adults. For instance, New York State's Educational Opportunity Program (EOP) and Higher Educational Opportunity Program (HEOP) offer grants to hard-knock kids like ours to go to state (EOP) schools or private (HEOP) colleges. We've jumped all over it because our kids, despite starting from a disadvantage, are highly competitive.

And highly adaptive. We've had kids who lived in group homes, or we've had to find homes for them. One of them, Mamadou

Dioum—"Dudu" to his friends—won a Group Home Person of the Year from Catholic Charities. The award came with a college scholarship, which Dudu took to New York Tech, where he became a civil engineer. Tell me that isn't a great story.

One day I got a call from Donna Lieberman, executive director of the New York Civil Liberties Union. It's a call that's all too familiar. "I need to get a kid out of the school he's in," she told me. The kid was Biko Edwards and he had been beaten up by a school safety agent in Canarsie, Brooklyn. That's right, he was beaten up by a *safety* agent. How abhorrent. Biko also needed a home. So, we arranged a safety transfer to King. And eventually something wonderful happened. He was taken in by the family of his teammate and good friend, Tetsu Yamada, a Japanese-American. How's that for your melting pot?

There will be more like Biko, because there will be more need.

In the early 1980s, I was on another sort of run: from the law. I was a fugitive, a junkie who had blown up his family, his teaching career, and his life savings. In one last desperate attempt at salvation, I returned home to New York. It welcomed me, like it does many strivers, and eventually returned me to the game I love.

It's that passion that keeps you alive. I'm now a seventy-something with a tricky ticker and Hep C, courtesy of my former drug use. But I get my old ass up in the morning and am glad to be able to see my team beat somebody. The feeling of winning is still incredible. And the feeling of helping is equally as rewarding, of knowing that these kids, at every level of their young lives, progress. In fact, we all need to have that. We need to have that empathy, passion, caring. We teach love; that love is soccer. We represent ethnic diversity and religious tolerance. We live in the most multicultural place on Earth and practice it. We play to win, but it's bigger than that.

The 2018 season ended in glory, but I am already looking forward to next season. My team is changing again. That's been one of the remarkable characteristics of New York City. Our ethnic history is a constantly changing patchwork of ethnicities. My first teams were dominated by kids from the islands—Trinidad and Jamaica. Then came the kids from Africa. As the freshmen appear each season, I can see where we're heading down the road. Next season it's going to be a group of Hispanic kids in leadership roles. They're going to be fabulous because of what they learned from the group before them, comprised mostly of African kids.

And to me, they could be from the island of purple. They could be from the island of pink. It matters not a whit to me where they're from, because a kid is a kid. And a gifted child in a sport needs a home and needs something to feel good about. I built an identity with these kids. We call it King Family.

On the field after we won the title, as we celebrated their championship, one of the school safety agents asked my assistant coach Josh Sherron: "What are you celebrating for, you win every year?" She didn't understand. It's so different from the inside. It takes an enormous amount of concentration and work. Many people, like Josh and my other assistant coaches, are dedicating their entire lives to making this thing happen. She didn't understand that part of what makes us so good is that our players are, in a way, not merely playing a game. They are playing for their futures.

# CHAPTER 2
# A King-dom Comes

HERE'S HOW YOU GET TO some of our home games if you play soccer for Martin Luther King High School in Manhattan. First, you get on the subway at 66th Street and Broadway, which is two blocks east of our school. You hop the No. 1 local train, take it one stop, then switch to the express train—the No. 2 or 3—at 72nd Street and take that train to 125th Street in Harlem.

Then you switch to the crazy bus.

That would be the M35 in the city's nomenclature of bus lines—the M is for Manhattan. But our kids have long called it the crazy bus. This is not a politically correct term, but they're still lacking in that kind of discretion at this point in their lives. And they do have a point.

Let me explain. The bus takes them across the Robert Kennedy (Triborough) Bridge, which spans the East River, and links the boroughs of Manhattan, Queens, and the Bronx. Sitting under that bridge is Randall's Island, where the Randall's Island Park Alliance, a private foundation, has built a wonderful complex of soccer and baseball fields, a tennis center run by John McEnroe's organization, a showpiece track and field stadium, a golf driving range, bike paths, and an environmental learning center.

But for much of New York City's history, Randall's Island, originally Blackwell's Island after one of its earliest colonial owners, has housed New York's discards. This policy was deliberate; the island provided isolation, the East River a moat. In colonial times, smallpox victims were sent here. The city bought Randall's outright in 1835 and has used it as a pauper's burial ground, the site of a poorhouse, a House of Refuge for juvenile delinquents, an Idiot Asylum for the mentally ill, a homeopathic hospital, and an Inebriate Asylum, to use the vernacular of the nineteenth century. In the twentieth century, the city and state built what are now called psychiatric hospitals but then called madhouses.

If we have a non-league Saturday game, the Department of Education doesn't want to give us subway passes. The kids have to pay it themselves, which really sucks. And so I go buy a bunch of Metro cards—subway tickets—that I give out. I'm not gonna let these kids use their last $2.50 or $5 for the day. They could feed themselves on that.

And after the subway ride comes the bus. For some background, Randall's and the now adjoined Wards Island still house the mentally challenged. There's even a prison hospital out there still, but in general there are group homes that deal with people who have mental disabilities, as well an outpatient facility. And, in New York, we've quite a few patients. So the only transportation outlet for these people is to jump on the bus, which picks them up right next to the field where we play, circumnavigates the island, and goes out back over the bridge, or vice versa. These folks are wild. They are not mentally disabled in terms of retardation, but mentally disabled emotionally. Their outbursts can be scary. And that's all we deal with. They're cursing, they're screaming, they're angry, they're potentially dangerous. And they're with us.

The general rule is that you don't engage. You have to just sit there with your mouth shut and try not to see what you're seeing and hear what you're hearing. And the kids, let's face it, they're New York kids. They learn to handle it. But this is what we go through to get to a game—not exactly a great warmup. I dare anybody to just try it once. And here they come running off the bus, over to the field, all of them together, off the M35. The famous M35.

We never did, and do not, have a field to call our home. The field we practice on is so bad that one of our goalkeeping coaches, Mickey Cohen, says he'd have never played on it, because he sees the kids get so beat up on it. And that's coming from a former pro goalkeeper. In the beginning we used garbage cans on a patch of dirt in Central Park for practice. On more than one occasion we have been escorted by the police or a security officer from private fields or fields where private schools had a permit. More recently I got a permit for a natural uneven surface field we call Goose Poop Field for obvious reasons.

Real estate has been getting scarcer and more expensive in Manhattan from the moment Peter Minuit bought it from Native Americans in 1626. Next season, though, we will be able to use a small practice field that is being built on campus. It's going to be a godsend to be able to keep the team on campus. In the outer boroughs, many schools have full-sized fields behind their buildings.

As usual, we fight for scraps. I first presented the idea to the Department of Education more than a decade ago. That's the way the bureaucracy grinds in a big city. Four years ago the project finally got the okay and the budget authorization. And now, after I have badgered enough politicians and found money from every possible source I could think of, the field will open in 2020. The Manhattan Borough President, Gale Brewer, says, "Martin Jacobson sends me more emails than anyone I know." Expect a lot more, Gale, because I will never cease advocating for education, and for our kids.

Which is to say that high school in New York City and high school soccer in New York City is not the same experience that most teenagers have across America.

For more than twenty years, I worked as a guidance counselor and soccer coach at what is now called Martin Luther King, Jr. Educational Campus. Although I am retired as a guidance counselor, I remain the co-athletic director. I have spent more than four decades as a teacher, counselor, dean, and administrator in public schools from Nanuet, New York, to Downriver Detroit to Santa Fe, New Mexico, and back to New York City. To say it's been a long, strange trip would be an understatement.

When I got to Martin Luther King, Jr. High in 1988, I was not hired to be a soccer coach and rain glory down on the school. Soccer was just another sport in this big, unwieldy comprehensive high school of three thousand students, and there were more pressing needs. I was brought on as a guidance counselor for English as a Second Language (ESL) students. In a city where some 40 percent of the inhabitants are foreign-born, you can imagine that there might be some demand. Maybe they thought that, because I had experience in New Mexico, I must speak Spanish. *Incorrecto. Yo comprendo español, pero hablo poquito,* I would always say. I understand Spanish, but speak just a little!

Nevertheless, working in ESL proved to be a wonderful occupation. Prior to that appointment I was working at Manhattan Center for Science and Math, and I was coaching at yet another school, La Guardia High School, which had a losing team and was playing in the city's B league. That is, it had a losing team until I got there. LaGuardia, which is New York's school for the performing arts, is directly across the street from King. I was also coaching girls' softball at LaGuardia, which was an interesting experience in itself. I had never coached cello players before.

Soon after I got hired at King, I ran into Maddy Yazwinski, who was the athletic director. She knew of my ability as a good coach and she told me, "I want to get you in here as soon as it opens up. I'd like you to take over the soccer team." Which turned out to be not too soon at all. I arrived at MLK in 1988; I was finally offered what turned out to be the job of my dreams as the soccer coach for MLK High School in 1994. In the meantime, the MLK soccer team continued in its own ramshackle fashion, losing more than winning, with coaching that was best described as disinterested. The year before I arrived, in fact, the team was winless.

Understand that teachers in New York City schools are unionized, and the rules require that you post any open positions. You have to post the soccer coach job in what they call a PERS session jump. It's a weird name for your typical New York City bureaucracy. A PERS session means there's a job opening that pays extra money, and that anybody in the building can apply. But there are rules. For instance, first, you have to be a phys ed teacher. The priority is going to be someone in the building, someone who's a phys ed teacher. And there I was, licensed in physical education and a counselor within the building.

When I got to King, it was a dysfunctional school with constant fights and other disruptions. But that didn't matter to me. Whatever they needed me for, I would do.

Because, before my life was nearly destroyed by heroin, I had risen to become a director of high school guidance at Santa Fe High School in New Mexico. And I was a good guidance counselor—even if I was the one who really needed guidance. But kids seemed to like me.

The reason, I think, is that I treat people—kids included—with respect. I have an open ear, and I'm a good listener—even though I can be a bit of a loud mouth. I can understand, I can empathize. I've gone through all different types of counseling training, from suicide prevention to child abuse to depression. I've got a master's in guidance counseling, and then I've got a post-master's certificate in alcohol and substance abuse counseling, which I never really used. I got offered some jobs, but I never took them.

You can take all the training you want and be certified in a lot of different behavior subspecialties but really, to be a counselor, you have to be empathetic. That starts with a term I use, civility. The kindness, caring. Caring about society. You've gotta care about society and its ills. So go ahead and tell me I'm a bit left wing—that's where I was in the seventies, actually, when I started realizing this was important. That we have to treat people right, we have to be kind to them.

And when I became a counselor to ESL students, I came into a world of people who very much needed kindness, because they didn't get enough of it where they came from. You hear stories about their path here, and some of them are frightening. I remember hearing one story about a girl who was tortured in her country in Africa. We got her legal aid to claim status as a refugee. She ended up getting her documents.

When you start working with ESL students, you find out that although the US is a much better place to live, the conditions can still be appalling, including the poverty that haunts their families from almost the moment they arrive. Their parents, if they are here, are people who are working hard, sometimes at the margins, to support their families. And on top of that, they're afraid of being deported. There are always these horrifying events that take place. I had one young man from Colombia whose house was raided by the drug enforcement agency (DEA). They took his dad away; and they put a gun to his head, in his mouth and told him they would kill him if he so much as breathed. Can you imagine how traumatic this is?

If you want to talk about living on the margins, then let me tell you about Mamadou Diop, who was a fixture on my championship team of 1997. He was another of the Senegalese kids who have long been anchors for my teams. He called me up one winter night, around midnight. He'd been working on 125th Street on the corner of 2nd Avenue—that's Harlem—in a fast food store selling fried fish. That's not unusual because our kids often have to work odd hours—that's what's available to them.

When Mamadou called, he was frantic. "Coach Jacques, please help me; come quickly." *M'aidez!* I hustled uptown to see a frightened, half-naked teenager. His store had been held up at gunpoint and the perps took his clothes off so he wouldn't run after them. As they say, you can't make this stuff up. And while the crime rate in New York has receded a lot since then, the danger still exists for some of these kids working odd hours in odd places.

While nativist ugliness is pouring out of the Trump administration, don't forget what happened to our world in the aftermath of 9/11. There was a kid from Mali, call him Ibrahim, one of the best to ever play for King. He almost never got here. He arrived as a kid with joy in his feet and heart, but without a home or a parent. We sent him to visit Macky Diop, another kid from Mali who had graduated King and was attending St. Lawrence College, near the Canadian border. We were working to get him into foster care in New York City. He was alone and living hand to mouth, more or less begging for accommodations and food among acquaintances. So Ibrahim headed off to visit this kid from Mali, so he could learn about establishing himself in America.

Ibrahim would soon learn about American justice and prejudice. As he was standing at the bus stop, getting ready to return home, he was swept off the streets by immigration agents. He was guilty of being too black, and too Muslim, in Canton, New York. Before we knew what was happening, our starting midfielder was taken to Buffalo. They then flew him from there to Atlanta. You can imagine how frightened this kid was, a million miles from home in a place filled with angry federal agents.

I began to reach out to everyone I thought could help. The FBI and INS weren't about to release him to me simply because I was down a midfielder. Through my growing network I was directed to a good lawyer, and after some considerable time, we were able to spring him. We lost him for the entire regular season, though. And clearly, you're not doing much training while in a federal lockup. But we managed to get him back in time for the playoffs. Oh, and he did manage to go on to have a professional career.

When I first got to King and began working with ESL kids, there was this feeling I had of a population that was so incredibly unique but one that also had special needs. Not like typical special needs students who are learning- or physically challenged, but special needs because they come from a culture that's so different than the culture in which we were brought up. I really started to feel for them, and it just evolved. You become who you are through caring. I just started caring right away with these kids.

Getting into the United States was easier then. There weren't a lot of requirements; you weren't treated like an enemy for wanting to live and work here. Kids weren't sent to jail by ICE at that time; they were sent to school. And when those kids got here, most of them just learned away.

Today, kids will still walk into my school. They're looking for me; they want to play on the team. But now I have to go through a whole different process, through high school admissions. That's the way the bureaucracy works, but at the same time it can work out. I get them in if I can. Every summer, club coaches will reach out to me because they want their best player to go to King. So do kids or their parents.

Funny thing is, although I worked for years in New Mexico, 1988 was my first year working with immigrants. Because in New Mexico, there weren't a lot of Mexicans coming over. Most of the Mexicans there were in fact Mexican-Americans just like any other hyphenated Americans.

I didn't know it at the time that I got to New York City, but I was about to get a great education on immigration law, social work, and the minutiae of government regulations. For instance, I didn't even know about green cards. I do now.

New York City offers school choice—it's very progressive in that way. So any child can choose to apply to any school within the five boroughs. It doesn't matter where you live. There are no zoning restrictions. Students get choices because the quality of education can vary tremendously within the city. Our top high schools, like Stuyvesant, are as good as any public or private schools in the country. But there are way too many failing schools. So the city offers choices, via a program that has been called Children First (or the School Choice or No Child Left Behind). This is all a part of the movement that kids should be allowed the best education that they can get.

Athletics is part of it. Kids who are good at basketball or baseball and angling for a college scholarship can choose the schools with the best athletic programs. And since we've had a great soccer team, kids want to come and play at MLK.

Over the last decade, something else has happened: the Department of Ed has redesigned the entire structure of the New York City school system, and King in particular. We're now called a campus, and each floor in our building has a different type of school and a different principal. A highly gifted student can apply to the Hunter Manhattan/ Hunter Science High School. Hunter, in fact, is one of the toughest schools to get into in the city because of its outstanding curriculum. And given that MLK is across the street from Lincoln Center for the Performing Arts, and New York is a media capital, we have schools that align students with those interests, such as the Maxine Greene School for Arts, Imagination and Inquiry, and the Special Music School High School. There's the Urban Assembly High School for Media Studies. There's the High School for Law, Advocacy, and Community Justice, and the High School for Art and Technology. This spreads the specialties around and also provides smaller learning communities so that kids, principals and parents, and teachers and administrators can work with four hundred or five hundred kids instead of three thousand.

So, in essence I get a crack at kids from six different schools. I have a guy who's a doctor now who came out of Hunter. He was another African—except he was Jewish and from South Africa as opposed to Muslim and from Mali. I have a player at the University of Pennsylvania right now and another who graduated from Cornell. Two youngsters are playing at St. John's, a top Division I program. We have players at all kinds of schools, from Borough of Manhattan Community College to state universities to St. Lawrence, Alfred, and the Ivy League. But the point is—they're all in school.

In the beginning, kids would come to MLK and ask for me. Their parents wanted them to play, but they also wanted them out of the neighborhood—even if King could be a rough place in itself. They became my Island boys. My first championship had seven Trinidadians—the Trinnies, I call them. These are kids that just came to the country and said, "Oh my God, there's a good coach in Manhattan. Let's go play for him."

In my first year at MLK soccer, the kids were excited to have a real coach. You can't fake that. Not only was I a real coach, but I was also a real loud coach, at least compared with what I am now—although some of the kids today would roll their eyes at that. Let's just say that I'm enthusiastic, boisterous. I was louder in those days, more boisterous because I had something to prove. I had to win for reasons unknown to a group of high schoolers. Bless them, the kids reacted positively. They didn't care because they took me for who I was, and because I gave them something—a drive, a will to win. Because I taught them drive and how to practice. Sometimes I worked so hard and got so excited that they would say, "Quiet, coach."

Eventually a couple of the kids came at me and said, "Can you not yell at us on the field?" That was difficult at first, but over the course of three or four years, I got better. Although I am still quite capable of getting in kids' faces if I think they need it. Just by learning more about the sport every day, and being willing to learn, you're able to change your tactics. You change. You're evolving; there's that word. I never ever stop learning.

From the beginning, though, they couldn't pronounce my name. The French-speaking kids from Africa would turn Jacobson into Jacques, or Jacka. That's how they kind of named me Jake, and I figured, why not?

So I became Coach Jake.

# CHAPTER 3
# What Makes a Coach?

I WANTED TO BECOME A coach in the worst way. Let me restate that a bit. The reason I became a coach is because I got to experience some truly awful coaches growing up. So clearly, I thought there was a low bar to success. But honestly, I knew at an early age that I could be better than those guys. That I could make a difference. And that I could win.

After being taught how to play soccer in my youth by the wonderful Herman Druckman—a German who spent a lot of his adult life in Brazil—I must have presumed that my high school coaches would be at least as good, even better. That thought process was brought to an abrupt end. Every year in high school I had a different coach, one worse than the other. The very worst was a fellow by the name of Mr. Ritaccio. He was a Latin teacher, Latin being a language requirement in those days. There are historical records of Romans kicking around pig bladders in a foreshadowing of what was to come, but Mr. Ritaccio had neither ancient nor current knowledge of soccer. He was picking up a paycheck.

Not having knowledge, not teaching fundamentals, not teaching the basics does not make a good coach, and Mr. R was all of that. Not taking an interest in you as an individual. All those things I felt were lacking in high school and college. Just a basic knowledge of the game. And knowing how to coach, teaching technique, giving me some pointers on strategy. How hard was that?

It would get even worse in college. My coach was a German guy named Neil Schmottlach, who was the polar opposite of Herman. Maybe the only living German who literally knew nothing about the game. Fortunately, Schmottlach had this guy named Arno Wittig as his assistant. He was a psychology professor who had played for Wheaton. He knew soccer. And I just wanted to be around him, instead of this Coach Schmottlach.

But how do you change the innate characteristics of the human who doesn't want to learn? Who doesn't have empathy, doesn't have caring, doesn't want to get into the kids' hearts? I've always felt there are so many groups of people in education who hate kids. I may sound narcissistic but, I'm telling you, there are so many people in public education who don't like kids. That, I just don't understand. Obviously, more do than don't—and there are many extraordinary teachers doing amazing things at our schools and all over the country. But there's still a high percentage of people—20 percent, 30 percent, I can't put a number on it because I've never done a study—who ought to be miners or in some other profession where compassion isn't a requirement.

In coaching, it's a similar story. You've got coaches who just want to go out there, not put in any extra time, any extra caring for a kid lacking in parents, a home, or emotional support. Will they go the extra mile to help that kid? And I think the word gets out that I care about young people. The individual. And I don't care about the kid just so the word gets out, I actually care about the kid.

We've got to change our society to care about children—for instance, not lock immigrant children up at the border. We've got to change our society to treat people with civility and kindness, and care about other people.

I got contacted by the coach of a team that was seeded rather high last year in the high school championship, but his team lost early in the tournament. Nicest guy in the world at a school out in Queens. He wanted to know: How do you do it, how do I build a team like yours?

And I think that's great. Here's a guy who wants to get better, willing to swallow his pride and ask.

In fact, I've done that all my life. I've asked people to help me get better as a coach.

Now, that happens to me. People ask, what does it take to do what you've done? Like a lot of things, there's no magic button, it's got to be innate, it's got to come from within. Someone can teach you how to play the piano, for instance, but not to become a pianist. You're going to have to want to become a better coach, you're going to have to want to become a better piano player, a better teacher, you're going to have to want to become a better auto mechanic. You've got to want it in life and if you don't, what purpose is there if you don't want to become the best at what you do?

So many coaches lack that purpose. Their purpose is a paycheck. Let's say you work all day as a biology teacher and a posting comes up—I can be the boys' soccer coach, girls' soccer coach, handball coach. God, look at this, I'm only making $46,000 a year. I can make another $6,000 if I coach, which isn't a hell of a lot, considering the taxes, but it's $6,000 more than I had. And all I have to do is show up for a few games, show up for practice, and maybe we'll kick a ball around.

Now, on the club soccer side, it's a different story, because parents are paying to have their kids coached. The clubs are more organized and you have directors of coaching—they have curriculums. These kids have wealthier parents who are going to demand that their kids be instructed. Our local clubs—Manhattan Soccer, Downtown United SC, Central Brooklyn—really adhere to curriculums and designs. Not that curriculums are perfect. But they adhere to a standard much higher than is required out of high school coaches in many ways. And that's a shame. Kids should have equal opportunity. Playing high school ball should not put you at a disadvantage because you can't afford to play for a private club.

When it comes down to it, the role is pretty simple. Recently, I went to watch our local MLS team, New York City FC, practice. They do the exact same thing I do. It's incredible. Or when I go to visit Nike, outside of Portland, I also catch up with my friend Gio Savarese, a New York City soccer legend who is currently the head coach of the Portland Timbers. What is he doing? In some contexts, it's fairly basic: small-sided games, putting the goal post together, stopping to do a little coaching, warming up guys with one-touch passing. It's not a difficult task to get a team out there and do some simple stuff.

Not only have I won 18 soccer titles, but as a wrestling coach for Stuyvesant High School I won two high school wrestling titles in 1990 and 1991. The banners are still on the wall. People don't realize it, but wrestling is really a mind sport. Stuyvesant is one of the city's top academic schools, and as I learned, it takes brains to be a wrestler. You have to be quick; the synapses have to work. Stuyvesant kids were perfect.

I wrestled at 140 pounds in high school. The appeal that wrestling had for me versus soccer was the head-to-head competition.

In the contrast to what I had in soccer, I had this great coach, Dave Finkle. I loved him. I was an okay wrestler but much better at soccer. Despite that, I learned that it's a good coach and a wonderful person—a kind person like Dave—who makes a difference. It so makes a difference when somebody cares about you.

There are very good high school coaches throughout the country who care. Who want to learn. I know that by being a member of the professional coaches association. There are just not enough of them. Throughout the New York City school system, there are extremely talented players. Plenty of them. So we should be losing more games than we do (we haven't lost in three years), but we don't.

How do you explain that?

For me, being a guidance counselor has been a critical piece of being a coach. I minored in psychology in college. I was curious about the mind as well as the body. That's the perfect combination. If you're a phys ed guy and a coach and have a counseling background—how much better does it get than that? That's why I got a degree in counseling. I also have a certification in alcohol and drug abuse. I really earned that latter one the hard way, given my previous addiction problems.

Now was I a great counselor? In some ways yes, and some ways I didn't really care. Truth be told, all I really cared about was coaching. Because when it came down to it, when someone asked what I did, I didn't say I was a guidance counselor. I said: I'm a soccer coach. One of my former principals who I just loved, Enid Margolis, would crack up and say: "Jake think he's a soccer coach." That said, I never short-changed a kid, not even one tenth. There isn't one kid in my life that didn't get the best of my ability. And I always treated every single parent with respect. To this day: I return every email or call.

I always did my job. Even back in my Santa Fe days, when I was a junkie, I was good at guidance because I was organized. Looking back, that's a strange duality: an organized junkie. But all I wanted to do is coach kids and use the counseling skills to help kids solve real problems. That was my goal, problem-solving.

The issue with guidance is that it is task-oriented to a fault. The guidance systems that I worked in aren't capable of telling kids how to change things to improve their lives. It's more like: How many credits do you have, how many do you need to graduate? Even though I had to do that bureaucratic stuff over the years, I have to admit that the more winning I did in soccer, the less I gave a crap about the bureaucratic aspects of counseling. What I really cared about was the development of these adolescent kids.

# CHAPTER 4
# College Boy

As A KID OF OUT of Brooklyn, you think you're tough enough and cool enough to handle yourself. And as an athlete, I was even more confident as I headed off to college in 1963. Especially since I was going to be attending school in the Midwest, at Ball State in Muncie, Indiana. The great Midwest. What could I possibly experience there that could be more challenging than living in metro New York?

Well, my visions of soccer glory would eventually be met with keen disappointment. My vision of college life in the sticks would be met with something quite different: sex, drugs, and rock and roll. I thought I was going to a place where I might see livestock. It turned out to be more Woodstock on the Prairie, and not in a good way.

Across college campuses nationally, the 1960s were a time of ferment, fury, and rebellion. The Greatest Generation had won the war, returned home to propagate the Baby Boom generation, and then watched in horror as their progeny rejected everything they cherished: their music, their sedentary suburban lifestyles, their willingness to become corporate drones, their no-sex-until-marriage prudishness, and their don't-question-authority ethos. The emergence of rock and roll, the British Invasion, the Motown Sound, folk rock, and other offshoots established a cultural barrier between the generations. The rising toll of the Vietnam War would galvanize college campuses into a political awakening. The wide availability of birth control pills started the sexual revolution, aided and abetted by the wider availability of illegal drugs: pot, LSD, uppers, downers, peyote. Not to mention that legal drug called alcohol. You name it—by the mid sixties, everything was available on every college campus in America.

Ball State was no different. Being in the heartland did not shelter Ball from the cultural revolution—hell, hemp grew wild along the roadsides—and it did not shelter me from the temptations of the late 1960s. I dove in with all the immaturity I could muster, which was considerable.

How did a 1960s city boy get to Ball State? Easy—by not trying. I had spent most of high school getting better at getting worse as a student. That had never stopped my parents or me from putting college in my future. My parents hadn't gone to college, nor had my older sister. Fulfilling the college dream—their college dream—was on my shoulders, and my parents had scrimped and saved for it. I had responded to their sacrifice and generosity by skipping school as much as I could.

I had co-conspirators in my truancy of course, in the form of my two buddies, Howie and Harry. Stupidly (how else would you describe it), we competed to see who could get the lowest grade point average. We were all hovering around 70 percent, which was a D. It wasn't that I lacked intelligence—I scored an 1100, about the 60th percentile, on my SAT without preparation—but I sure lacked motivation. My life was about soccer, wrestling, friends, and girls.

My knowledge of Ball State was minimal, which is fitting, as it matched my knowledge about just about everything. Indiana—was that part of Iowa? But I knew Ball State had a soccer team that was eager to have me.

Plus, Howie and Harry decided to go along for the ride. They applied after they learned that there was a school that would actually take me. We three launched our college careers and adult lives in the summer of 1963 as we headed to Indiana for orientation, a Midwestern shakedown cruise for the three East Coast Jews. We boarded a train at

Grand Central Station—I'm not sure Muncie even had air service—
and settled in, three urbanites and dummies, classic New York wise-
asses. On the way to Muncie, we discussed girls and sports; we dissed
other people on the train. As the train made its way West, the dense
urban environment that we left gradually gave way to the vastness of a
landscape that stretched to the horizon.

We arrived in Muncie in early afternoon and were immediately
shown to a dormitory. We took a few minutes to unpack, then headed
downstairs to the student union for a soda. Horseplay ensued almost
immediately, as we ended up playing bumper cars with a couple of
large-wheeled dollies smashing property that wasn't ours. It was
great. If this was a preview of college, I thought, bring it on. Then
someone tapped me on the shoulder. It was the campus police. They
led us to their office and gave us a reprimand. I'd like to say that we
took the police seriously, but they seemed like a bunch of hayseeds.
I'm sure we were as strange to them. Overall, it was an inauspicious
start.

We returned from orientation to New York, and I'm sure it must
have thrilled my parents to hear me tell them how great Indiana was,
and how excited I was to be a frosh at Ball, bumper car incidents notwithstanding. They were relieved and proud. Their son, the college
boy. My mother sewed labels in all my shirts. That September, we
packed into my father's car and headed for Hoosierland.

The trip was a major milestone for my parents, too. They had traveled to the famous Jewish resorts of the Catskill Mountains, of course,
but I don't think they had ever been farther west than Monticello,
New York. My father was in decent health at that time, and he did all
the driving. I'll never forget the drive, in part because I'll never forget
the car—it was a Studebaker Lark, a car that was advertised as "The
Compact with Performability." It was even more compact on that trip.
My belongings filled the back seat and trunk, so the three of us were
wedged into the front seat. We couldn't afford to stop along the way
for overnight stays, so we drove straight from Long Island to Indiana.

In those days that was no short haul; the interstate highway system was still in its infancy.

My parents helped me unload my belongings at Wagoner Hall, one of the big dormitories on campus, then headed back to the Studebaker. At least they'd be more comfortable and less compact on the ride home. I met my roommate, a tall skinny kid from Northern Indiana named Michael. While we were filling my bathroom medicine cabinet with the usual toiletries—toothpaste, deodorant, soap—Michael's side of the medicine cabinet was empty. After a little while I realized that it reflected his Christian Scientist beliefs. The culture shock was intense—I understood Christian Science about as well as he understood Judaism—and I don't think it subsided for either of us. We got along well enough, but we were never going to be friends. We were from two different planets. That was not the case with all of the folks at Ball State, who were easy to get along with, friendly, and forthcoming.

The go along/get along relationship with Michael ended abruptly on November 22, 1963, as I was getting ready to go home for Thanksgiving break. He burst into the room and said, "Guess what? Kennedy's dead." I was starting to respond when I saw that his expression wasn't one of shock or sadness. "Isn't that great?" he said. Now, I may have been a guy from New York more concerned with sports and girls than with national politics. Still, New York loved Kennedy. Jewish New York, a traditionally Democrat bloc, loved Kennedy. And so, especially, did Irish New York, since Kennedy was an Irish-American Catholic—the apparent source of Michael's hatred.

Any American alive then can tell you still today where they were and what they were doing at the moment they heard the news. I can tell you that I was ready to beat the crap out of Michael for those hateful words. I rushed him and shoved him to the ground; I could have killed him, but the shock of the day perhaps drained my anger enough. When I got back to New York, the city was in mourning, as was the country. Going back to Wagoner Hall and living peacefully with my Christian Scientist roommate did not seem possible, nor desirable.

I was saved by Greeks. Fraternities were big at Ball State, and I was in the gym when several upperclassmen approached me. They were from Sigma Tau Gamma, one of the animal fraternities, which is what they called the frats heavy on athletes and partiers. I fit in perfectly with those reprobates and they asked me to pledge. (By comparison, David Letterman, who was at Ball State at the same time that I was, joined a Sigma Chi, where the dorks hung out. Funny. Our paths never crossed.) By my freshman spring, the fraternity became the center of my social life and even my residential life—I ditched the dorm and moved into the frat house. The parties then began in earnest, with lots of drinking and the usual stupid frat behavior.

But it was not totally without educational benefit—it's where I learned about sex. My experience with my high school girlfriends was more about effort than success. Then came that cold spring night during my freshman year of college. One of the brothers had a car, a ten-year-old Buick, an absolute land yacht where I would have my first real sexual experience.

Suddenly (and you can take that any way you want), the world became a different place. For the first time in my life, I understood the pull of sex, wholly and irreversibly. It would be one of the things that shaped what was an addictive, compulsive personality. One of those things—sports—would turn out to be beneficial. The other—drugs—would turn out to be a disaster. The story of that infamous car continued long after my evening with Betty. The guys in the frat nicknamed the Buick the "Hummermobile," and a few years later took it to Daytona Beach for spring break. A local news photographer thought the car, labeled with its nickname, was amusing enough to take a picture, which made the front page of the local paper. Crazy college kids.

There would be many more hookups my freshman year. So many women. My attentions were hardly being diverted by academics though; I was coasting from the moment I arrived. The coursework was pretty undemanding—general liberal arts with some physical education instruction. Plus, I felt like the New York education I got—at least when I showed up—had given me a real edge. These kids were from graduating classes of twenty or thirty at most and had been taught by teachers from places like, um, Ball State. The schools in New York were large and highly competitive, and the parents were demanding. My senior class had almost four hundred kids, and many of my high school teachers had advanced degrees.

As unchallenging as Ball State was, I didn't exactly rise to it. Normally, I would have poured all my energy into sports, but my athletic career was on hold. The soccer program was run by a guy named Chuck Fairbanks, and I didn't have much confidence in him as a coach. Besides, this was still the era when freshmen couldn't play varsity, so I decided to sit out the first year. I still played club and intramural sports, though: baseball in the quad and flag football. That first winter, in fact, I broke my arm stretching out for a long pass and had to wear a cast.

The cast was always a way to start a conversation with girls ("yeah, broke it playing football"), and though my academic and athletic life may have been sidetracked, my social life was roaring. A pattern was quickly established: go to party, meet girl, take girl home. Or maybe go to bar, meet girl, take girl home. It was a song with any number of intermezzos but only one coda.

And what was it about these Indiana women? Had they learned about sex growing up on farms watching the cows and the pigs and the birds and the bees do it? Just who was the rube here?

Getting women became something more than a pastime; it was almost an obsession. There was no need to have steady girlfriends—I was with one girl for a week or two, and then I moved on, or she did. Back in New York, no one had sex—at least no one I knew. As far as I knew, the girls in my high school were virgins. In Indiana, sex was everywhere.

Although every Jewish mother wants her boy to settle down with a nice Jewish girl, let's just say that I was ecumenical regarding sex. Not that I wasn't reminded of my Jewishness. I remember going to a study hall with a pretty girl I wanted to impress. We were taking a history class together, and all of a sudden she pointed at something on the page and mumbled a couple of words. I wasn't paying attention: I was probably looking at her body, or thinking of touching her body. "What?" I asked.

"I don't know why they don't mention it here," she said.

"Mention what?"

"The fact that Jews have horns."

I was dumbfounded. She actually thought Jews had horns growing out of their heads, like cartoon devils. This might have been a moment to dispel these hateful stereotypes, but I was not going to put cultural exchange ahead of intercourse. Sorry, Rabbi. Later that week, I got the girl who thought Jews had horns into bed. The next week, I moved on to another girl, a little redhead who had grown up downstate. And then, about two weeks after that, there was a tall brunette girl who had moved all around because her father was in the military.

This was obsessive-compulsive, addictive behavior. When I think about it now, it sounds insane. There had to be fifty or sixty women of every type imaginable—classmates, locals, barflies, prostitutes, women at the bottom of the barrel and women who were out of my league. I was a sexual revolution of one.

Sigma Tau Gamma not only introduced me to sex, it also threw in booze. Naturally. They go together in college. Once again, Indianans would surprise me with their robust appetite for decadence. They drank, all the time, everywhere, to excess. I suppose this was going on at college campuses spread across the country. But there were no such sprawling college campuses where I grew up.

And as I was in Rome (albeit the Midwestern section), I did as the Romans did. I went to parties, drank so much beer I thought I'd explode, and then drove drunk along poorly lit country roads. I went to sleep drunk, let the alcohol drain out, and woke up feeling great. College was like an endless carnival. To be honest, I don't think I was addicted to the alcohol. It was a social high. I drank because everyone else around me was drinking.

The drugs started much the same way.

I had my first joint as a freshman, too. An upperclassman from Chicago offered it to me at a party and I accepted. I wasn't the kind of kid who said no to things like that. I lifted the joint to my lips and took a drag. Nothing. Maybe a little high, but I didn't see what all the fuss was about. There was no buzz or brain alteration in any major way. Later, I would come to understand that it was probably because the quality of the marijuana wasn't very good. At the time, I just shrugged, put the joint down, and went back to drinking.

My friends really didn't see much difference in the guy who returned from Ball State to New York that summer. Sure, I was a college guy and sexually experienced, but I returned to the world I left. I hung out with high school friends, compared notes on our college experiences, and went to parties. The major difference was that I tried to pick up girls whenever possible. At that I succeeded. Back in 7th or 8th grade, I had met and befriended a pretty girl at one of the beach clubs on Long Island. That first summer back from college, I ran into her in town and ended up sleeping with her. It never would have happened to the younger me. It was a way of marking myself as a man. And yet, it was a girl I had known in youth—mature and childish all at once. That was very exciting for me.

But summer also introduced me to work—I had to earn money for college. My Uncle Joe, my mother's brother, was a factory foreman, and he got me a job at Lieb Ironworks in Jamaica, Queens. I made fire escapes, which every tenement in New York has to have. Every morning, I woke up early, drove out to the ironworks, put in a full day, and then came home. Manual labor was exhausting. After a week of that kind of physical drudgery, I couldn't wait to get back to college. This was a cruel reversal: some kids worked hard all year and got to take the summers off. I joked around and partied the entire year and then was sold into hard labor during the summers. I worked at the ironworks for three summers, in fact, right up until the moment that I saw my Uncle Joe drop dead of a brain hemorrhage on the job. But I already figured out that the only thing keeping me from a lifetime of factory work would be a college degree.

That first summer, I also started to prepare myself for soccer. There was a kid named Phil who was a year behind me in school, and toward the end of my freshman year he decided that he was going to join us at Ball State. He was yet another member of the elite seventy-grade-point-average club. So when I returned after freshman year, I spent lots of time telling him about what he could expect in the way of girls, sports, and classes. Phil was also a soccer player, and the two of us would go out to the beach on the weekend and practice shots for hours in the sand. It was great training, and when I arrived back in Muncie for sophomore year, I was ready.

The only problem was that they weren't ready for me. Chuck Fairbanks, who had been the coach my freshman year, had left the school. Chuck was certainly no coaching genius, but his successor made him look like Sir Alex Ferguson. He didn't know anything about kids, and he certainly didn't know anything about the sport. Some of the players responded by growing disillusioned, but I was a cocky New Yorker, and I spent much of my time talking back to my new coach. I wouldn't have survived at all, except that I was a good player, much better than most of the guys who came out for the team.

As a Ph.D., Coach knew a lot about something, but he knew nothing about soccer. This was the old days of soccer formations, predominated by a 2-3-5 setup, with five strikers: a center forward, inside right, inside left, outside right, outside left. Behind them were three midfielders and then two fullbacks. The game we played back then had lots of little passes between players to no real effect; mostly it was kick and run, kick and run. That would change when the Dutch introduced a revolutionary concept called Total Football in the late 1960s that would allow any player to sweep forward in possession. The old standard formation has evolved to 4-2-3-1, or 4-3-3 among others, allowing teams to exploit both space and speed. The game our kids at MLK play today is much more beautiful, full of open spaces and lyrical passages. They would have killed my Ball State team.

I played center forward—the star man. Ball State was in a strange circumstance regarding soccer. We were in the Midwestern League along with Michigan State and St. Louis, which were both national soccer powerhouses at the time, even competing for the national championship. Our team had one kid from Egypt, some local kids who weren't bad, and a good player from New York named Butch Jacobson.

That was me; I was still a long way from being Jake. Butch was a nickname I had gotten from my Uncle Joe, and it stuck to me for much of my childhood and my early athletic career. A few games into the season, it was clear how the matches would play out: we'd be competitive against the weaker teams and get flattened by the good teams, the teams with real coaches. That's pretty much how it went. There were some bright spots for me. Most memorably, I scored two goals in a 4–2 loss to Indiana.

Playing for a varsity team in a small Midwestern city affords a college student one small luxury: visiting other Midwestern cities. Our team would travel to Northern Illinois, down to Missouri, up to Michigan. We weren't the big men on campus like the football team or the basketball team—those were dominant sports in Indiana, and still are. Even the volleyball team, which was surprisingly successful, enjoyed a big following on campus. But as varsity athletes, we still had status. It was something I could be proud of. I had an identity. I could walk into the gym and people would know exactly who I was.

My parents even got a chance to see me play. They flew to Akron, Ohio, where we were scheduled to play against the Akron Zips before a college football game. That made for a huge crowd, and I scored a goal. My dad came West by himself and watched me play in a home game against Northern Illinois, in DeKalb. That's one of my fondest college memories. The game occurred during a period where my father hadn't been well at all. I was happy to see him and also eager to make him proud. It showed in my play, and then, in the second half, I scored on a spectacular bicycle kick. Afterwards, our idiot coach came over and told my dad what a great job I had done, and that he was sure that I had a future in the sport. It's a sentimental memory, but I have so few memories of my dad from that time that I hold onto it tightly.

Mostly, though, we were doomed by a dearth of talent and tactics to playing mediocre soccer in front of a few dozen fans. To keep ourselves entertained, we clowned in the locker room, on the field, and especially on the team bus, in light of how long we spent on the road. Fittingly, given the times, we began to clown around with drugs.

Not necessarily the kind you're thinking about. Phil and I drank over-the-counter Robitussin. In those days, cough medicine ingredients routinely included codeine. No one ever suspected us, and certainly no one ever caught us. We were also getting high from Benzedrex inhalers, used to treat allergy or sinus problems. Propylhexedrine, a synthetic stimulant similar to methamphetamine, is the active ingredient. We'd crack the inhalers open, extract the propylhexedrine-soaked cotton, cut it up, and drink it with Coca-Cola. It was a minor high, but when you belched, you really felt it—the Benzedrex coming back up with the pieces of cotton was painful. Amphetamines were another popular drug of choice—and common then. My mother used them for weight loss. At school, students took them for concentration, or to stay awake and study.

We had no remotely noble purpose such as studying. We were just getting high. When it came time for the game, we straightened out and went to play. Although the collegiate drug scene was expanding nationally, at Ball State the drug of choice was still alcohol. There was no cocaine, no LSD, no Quaaludes, no heroin. We were insulated. We were dumb. And we were happy.

That seemed like the whole point of college. Once I went to a party at a different frat house, and afterwards, a few friends and I ended up drinking and smoking dope in the street. I was taking a course in the fundamentals of basketball at the time, and at the end of the next week, we got our grades for the quarter. The teacher gave me a C, which surprised and hurt me. He had loved having me in his class. I was one of his prized pupils. I went to his office and said, "What's with the grade?"

He wagged his finger at me. "I saw you," he said. "I saw you outside of that party."

I could have stopped and thought about what he said. I was a varsity athlete, after all. Maybe it made sense for me to set a better example. But this is not how you react as a rambunctious collegian. Instead, I went back to the frat house, complained about the professor—how he was judging me through the prism of his conservative Midwestern Christian values—and poured myself a Seagram's 7.

# CHAPTER 5
# Adulthood in Nanuet

THE LOOMING END OF THE college cocoon makes most seniors a little wistful as well as slightly anxious. And why wouldn't they be? Ball State in the late 1960s might have been a bit of an unusual choice for a New York kid, but it felt as comfortable as an old couch for me. I had soccer, I had sex, and I had a social life. I had no trouble keeping up in class. But I didn't have a real girlfriend and I didn't have a real way to continue my connection to the college after graduation.

A woman named Tanya solved that problem beautifully. She was a freshman, a brunette teenager from Indiana. Lovely. We met as spring approached and the relationship flowered quickly.

She would be ample reason to return to campus next semester, from whatever job that awaited me. With graduation in sight for me, Tanya stopped by unexpectedly. "I have some news," she said. "I'm pregnant." You're what? The sixties may have been the Free Love generation, but birth control was not widely available, nor practiced—at least Tanya and I weren't practicing it. Out-of-wedlock pregnancies were still relatively rare and tainted by shame. Abortion in Indiana was even less available than it is now. When Tanya told me she was pregnant, we knew that we'd have to get married. This was the expected behavior. I had to man up and be a father.

My parents were aghast. They certainly wanted grandchildren at some point. Jewish grandchildren, to be more specific, and Tanya was WASP squared. She hailed from a privileged background and a wealthy, cornbread family. Which is to say that her family was also anti-Semitic (sadly familiar in Indiana then) and less than excited about the fact that their daughter had been knocked up by a New York Jew. But marrying a Jew was apparently less shameful than being an unwed mother, and so it was that the two sets of parents had what I suppose was a dreadful conversation about our futures. When my parents came out for my graduation, they met. I suppose things could have gone worse, although I'm not sure how.

Our parents got along like pastrami and mayonnaise. That is to say, they didn't go together well. Hers were probably in this country for two hundred years and were landed gentry. Mine were one generation from off the shtetl and off the boat. This was not going to be the little melting pot on the prairie.

Lacking an alternative, we got hitched in a ceremony that was civil, but barely. By that I mean, I wouldn't let a minister marry us, so we found a justice of the peace. Whatever thoughts I had entertained about enjoying the single life as a twenty-something faded like Ball State in the rearview as we packed up and drove home. Clearly I would have to get a job to support the child that was on the way. That secured, Tanya would then join me. And the baby would make three. My mother, then in full Jewish Mother mode, took immediate charge of my life. She helped me find an apartment, and when I did we drove to Flatbush Avenue in Brooklyn to buy a bedroom set.

New York's suburbs were still growing like kudzu then. Teachers were needed everywhere, including Nanuet, New York, which is about twenty miles north of Manhattan and just north of the New Jersey border. It had a shopping mall. I suppose it was as boring as any other suburb, but at least it was close to the Big City. My mother was again riding shotgun, sitting in the waiting room while I applied for the job.

Even then, my people skills were excellent. I knew how to engage interviewers and I ended up getting offered a spot at a middle school, where I would also be responsible for coaching wrestling and soccer.

Apartment? Check. Job? Check. Wife and child? On the way. Tanya and I talked often, like a couple of newlyweds making plans for the future. I started to believe what I had with her. And I was acting the part, having toned down the drinking and drugs, because a family man doesn't do that stuff.

And then the family arrived—or at least Tanya did, delivered by her mother. She hadn't forewarned me. I came home from work to find them parked outside my apartment complex. My erstwhile mother-in-law was as frigid as an Indiana winter to me as she dropped her daughter off. There have been friendlier hostage exchanges. Nevertheless, Tanya and I had an emotional reunion. She was four to five months pregnant. Our lifelong adventure, it seemed, had just begun.

Or maybe our month-long adventure. Tanya, a Midwesterner through and through, felt like an alien in New York. She didn't like it very much, and after a while, she didn't like me. She hadn't made any close friends, which caused her to spend more and more time on the phone with her mother, racking up considerable bills in the process. I could hardly complain. She was lonely and needed to discuss things with her mother. Such as leaving me, it turns out. I came home from work one day to find her sitting in the living room. "Why aren't you on the phone talking to your mother?" I said.

"Not necessary," she said, pointing to the bedroom. "She's in there."

"What is she doing?" I asked.

"Packing my things," she said.

There wasn't going to be a long goodbye, nor was I doing much to talk her out of it. I'm not really sure I wanted to try. It was awkward enough to carry her things to the car, where Tanya had retreated, staring straight ahead. I no longer existed as of that moment. And shortly thereafter, neither did our marriage. My mother made sure of it by having the marriage annulled. That was not such an easy thing to do given Tanya's pregnancy, but my mother, ever the fighter, got a New York judge to free me from matrimony.

Whatever I had envisioned about living an Ozzie and Harriet, *Leave It to Beaver* lifestyle left that night. Little did I know that I would never have it. There would be more matrimonial hell to pay in the future.

But this was crushing. The woman who was going to bridge me from college to adulthood had burned the bridge. And Tanya was not the only thing that was going: so was my hair. I had been dreading this since I was in high school. I first noticed it when I was about sixteen. One evening I had been doing homework and I put my head in my hands to concentrate. When I took my hands of my head, I was horrified to see that some of my hair stayed there. Michael Jordan was not yet on the scene to make baldness badass. In the age of the Beatles, this was fashion tragedy. Worse, this was going to make me less attractive to women now that Tanya was gone.

Living alone in Nanuet made me at least understand Tanya's misery. She was alone all day, and living alone in Nanuet was like living in a penal colony. I called my sister, Marsha, and begged her to let me crash in her apartment until I could get myself straightened out a bit. She shared an apartment on Park Avenue in Manhattan—civilization—with a roommate. I was an original couch surfer long before millennials invented it. Except that I had a job and reverse commuted across the George Washington or Tappan Zee Bridge to Nanuet.

That forty-five-minute commute followed by classes and coaching left little time but work, couch, work, couch. The buzz of Manhattan couldn't do much to counter the loneliness and loss I was feeling. Despite the imminent birth of our child, Tanya and I did not communicate.

Getting to work with kids was a tonic. They needed me; they responded to me. And I found a great mentor named Ray Stedge. I would learn how important mentorship can be. I also learned that I loved teaching and coaching; and I *really* loved winning. Not that my teams were so great. But when we did win, I began to understand the feeling of victory—how powerful it could be for a group of athletes, how it could motivate and clarify and improve how they perform.

Maybe it was that winning feeling that prompted me to get off the couch, so to speak, and move back to Nanuet. My sister didn't protest when I told her I was returning to the scene of my matrimonial crime. She'd already put up with me for three months and the commute seemed to be getting longer. My reentry came via a rooming house near the school. My rental had a sink and a color TV that was my prized possession. The toilet was down the hall. Price: twenty bucks a week. My life now was hardly a glamorous, or even interesting, routine—home, work, the occasional pizza out—but having any routine was good after the trauma of the last six months.

My routine was interrupted one day by one of the other tenants. "Hi," he said. "I'm Ronnie."

"Nice to meet you," I said. I'm a talker, that I can tell you. So I bummed a cigarette off of him and we smoked and talked. Ronnie claimed to be an inventor and a mechanic, a tinkerer who, he bragged, wouldn't be around long after one of his crazy ideas for machines that would change the world would make him rich. Ronnie was good for a laugh, even if his money-making machine never materialized. What did materialize one day was a joint. He casually asked me if I got high and I told him, "Sure." Hell, I went to college, didn't I? Cigarettes were replaced by joints that we would smoke in my room.

Our routine would continue like that until Ronnie asked if I wanted to step up my game—did I want to try heroin? To this day I haven't figured out why I didn't translate those words into, "Would you like to risk your future and your life for five minutes of bliss?" My answer was on the order of, "Sounds like a good deal."

Ronnie was fully equipped. He provided a needle with a plunger on the top. You insert the needle under the skin surface and then depress the plunger. The heroin forms a small blister-like bubble just beneath the skin and gets absorbed gradually. This is skin-popping, which is safer than mainlining—not that I had a clue at that time.

I received a not-so-subtle message the first time Ronnie shot me up. The incredible euphoria I was expecting went immediately sideways, and I puked. My body was telling me something. But I wasn't listening. The same thing happened the second time. That didn't stop me from trying again until I could at least tolerate heroin. I would use it occasionally, but school was taking up most of my time and interest.

One day, I came back from work and noticed that the door to my room, which I locked every day, was wide open. Maybe Ronnie was hanging out watching my television. "Ronnie," I called. No answer. I stepped inside and realized Ronnie wasn't watching my television because my very expensive color television was gone. Ronnie said he hadn't taken it—hey, he was my friend—but he hung with people who didn't have a second thought about stealing a friend's television to buy another bag. Junkies have no real friends other than junk. Another lesson not learned. But at least I was smart enough to move to another rooming house, one free of criminals.

Meanwhile, Ball State was not done playing with my heart. Whatever the damage inflicted by Tanya, I still had great affection for the college—and especially its women. Janet was one of them. I had known her at Ball State, but not well, and certainly not intimately. In a relatively small place like Ball, you get to know a lot of people. Like Tanya, she was Hoosier through and through, from Knox, Indiana. Unlike Tanya, she hailed from less exalted family stock. Her father was a postmaster, her mother the dutiful housewife. You can imagine the white picket fence around the house. We reconnected with each other in the spring of 1969, after I saw her mentioned in *Ball State Magazine*.

Neither of us had fully dialed into living like adults. Maybe that's why we came up with a plan to drive to Florida for college spring break. There could hardly be anything less mature, less adult to do than hang out in Fort Lauderdale (aka Fort Liquordale) or Daytona, absorbing sunshine and beer in no particular order. One of my friends, Harry, decided to join us. Rather than fly directly to Florida, Janet flew to New York. Road trip!

It wouldn't be all that long before Janet and I were on the road to romance, and then commitment. Within a few months, Janet decided to move East to live with me. Unlike Tanya, she was looking forward to a new setting and a new life. And she had chosen me; this was not a matter of social mores forcing a marriage.

Janet, who had studied social work, also found a job in the public sector. She became a probation officer in Rockland County, while I kept teaching and hopefully creating the kinds of young adults who wouldn't need Janet's professional guidance. We married that winter of 1970. She wasn't interested in a traditional wedding. Her parents came out from Indiana with a few of their friends. My mother capped the list at twenty people.

My dad's health was deteriorating rapidly, but he was able to make the wedding and make a toast. His diabetes was now setting off serial medical events: a stroke and several minor heart attacks. Later that year he was hospitalized yet again, so Janet and I went to stay in Long Beach with my mother. We were eating dinner with my mother when we got a call from the hospital. My dad had suffered a heart attack; he couldn't be resuscitated. We're so sorry. He was fifty-three.

I suppose I knew he was dying, but some part of you thinks that day won't come. At least not today. Or tomorrow. Then it does. The loss is raw, gaping. Decades would pass before I could fully come to terms with it.

There were other grownup issues to deal with, too. The Vietnam War was entering what would be its final phase, at least in terms of American involvement, and anti-war protests were still raging. No one wanted to fight this war any more. In response to criticism that college deferments allowed wealthier kids to avoid the draft, the government ended the practice. Instead, everyone draft-eligible (males born between 1944 and 1950) would be entered in the lottery. Only in this case, the winners were the losers. The Selective Service used randomly selected birthdates to determine draft order. If your birthdate was among the first one hundred birthdates selected, you were as good as drafted. Being able to watch this take place on television was unnerving. But my birthday came up at 330, which meant that I wasn't going anywhere.

And that in itself was a problem. Janet and I were young and restless, and in keeping with the times were not going to settle down into the same middle-class humdrummery that our parents had embraced. The members of the Greatest Generation who had lived through the Depression and survived the war were going to live happily ever after in the Nanuets and Levittowns of America. Their offspring made no such deal and, somewhat predictably, rejected everything their parents cherished.

Janet and I were part of that vanguard. We pooled our money, raided our retirement funds, and bought a pop-top camper that I painted red, white, and blue, with a peace sign for extra decoration. Ken Kesey was going to have nothing on us. We hitched the camper to the back of my white Ford Fairlane, and ditched Nanuet.

# CHAPTER 6
# Mellow in Muncie

WE WERE NOT SURE WHERE we were headed, other than westward.

The routine would be blissfully simple. Drive to campground, where we'd run into young people like ourselves who were escaping the rat race even before it started. Like us, they would have amphetamines to help them drive and marijuana to help them socialize. Not what you think of when Yellowstone comes to mind, but America in 1970 was a different place.

When we reached Sawtooth National Forest in Idaho, I had a life-changing event. I parked the car, hopped out, and looked up into the most beautiful national park I had ever seen. It was a cathedral of enormous trees, the sky beyond them the deepest blue I had ever seen.

For me, it would begin a lifelong love affair with our national parks, one that would endure throughout my somewhat chaotic life. I've had a chance to visit nearly every national park, hike through them for days on end. If you want to find tranquility, believe me—take a hike.

That day in Idaho, I also discovered that things grow in the forest. As in marijuana plants the size of pine trees. Clearly, they had been planted by pot dealers, a practice that has been an ongoing issue for forest managers in places like Humboldt National Forest in California. I did some weeding: I pulled the marijuana plants up, hung them upside down, and let them dry. I then placed them in the trunk of my car.

As we crossed into California from Oregon, we were stopped at the border roadblock by people in uniforms. I was terrified, thinking we'd be busted for possessing marijuana and hauled off to jail. To my utter relief, the cops were from the California Department of Agriculture. We had been pulled over by the fruit and vegetable patrol, the produce police. They peeked in the car, spotting only a suspicious watermelon in the back seat. The melon got a pass; so did we. "Go on through," the inspector said, smiling.

The California that we entered was the hippie paradise I'd only ever read about in *Rolling Stone*. Sex, drugs, and dancing in the street. And that gorgeous coastline. That first weekend, we headed into Santa Barbara. That's where I dropped acid for the first time. The experience, I must admit, was great—what an awareness of nature, what euphoria. Janet fared far worse—a bad trip—but she promised me she'd try again. There would be plenty of opportunities.

We probably would have stayed in California forever but for the inconvenience of running out of money. That left us a choice of going back East to New York, to conventional living. But that thought was depressing enough. Nanuet? No way.

There are two ways to avoid adult responsibilities when you are that young. The first is to hang out until your money runs out. The second is grad school, where you can hang out like you hung out as an undergrad. The difference is that you are a more experienced student. Janet had the idea that we could avoid capture by returning to Ball State. If I could earn a master's degree, I could qualify for a better job. We still had friends there, too.

Ball State accepted me into its graduate program. We upgraded from our undergrad days, getting a small elegant apartment in a Victorian house on Riverside Drive in Muncie for $250 a month. I enrolled to get a master's in guidance and counseling. My teaching experience enabled me to get a job working for a program called Deferred Admissions Student Experimental Program, or DASEP. The idea was to help inner-city kids from urban areas such Gary and Indianapolis acclimate to college life.

My employment was a product of affirmative action in reverse: the program heads had to hire at least one white counselor. I was a token. And toking. The black grad students I worked with were always stepping out of the office to light up a joint. And they were kind enough to invite their token along. These guys and girls had a grade of marijuana that was much better than what I could get in Muncie: Panama Red, gourmet stuff. As a pothead, I was a bit of a cliché: mellow, forgetful, and afflicted by the munchies. Doughnuts solved that last problem and created another one. My weight soared forty or fifty pounds to around 195 or 200. That didn't matter. Nothing did. I was mellow in Muncie.

My friend Harold did not escape the draft like I did. He had, like thousands of other unfortunate young men, been sent off to Vietnam to fight what had become an extremely unpopular war. But at least he got back alive, if yet not quite whole. He resettled in California, although perhaps "unsettled" is more like it. I had known him in college when he was just one of a lot of skinny, long-haired students. Nam had transformed him. When he returned to visit campus in October of 1970, he was a complete hippie as well as anti-war, anti-government, anti-establishment, and very angry.

We smoked joints, talked about the war, dropped acid, and talked about the president. As far as I'm concerned, Harold could have been one of the first conspiracy buffs, with theories about everything. He had a business plan, too, to import California dope to Indiana. He would, of course, need a sales force, which is where I came in. "You help me sell it and I'll give you all the dope you can smoke," he said.

Being a small-time pot dealer in an insulated college town doesn't constitute a big operation. Within weeks, I was dealing marijuana out of the house on Riverside Drive. I was selling mostly to friends and co-workers to get the free dope that Harold had promised. But it boosted my status on campus, since inevitably, Harold upgraded the product mix. He was flying back to California from one of his trips when he met a chemist on the plane. A chemist and opportunist. The chemist knew how to take lysergic acid diethylamide and dip blotter paper with a picture of Mr. Natural into it. Blotter acid, in the trade. It was like manufacturing money.

Harold was also a master ripoff artist, a skill he honed to show his contempt for corporate America. I learned how to steal credit card numbers on the phone, how to make phony credit card applications, and how to scam rental car companies. I once challenged him while sitting in our apartment smoking joints about his virulent anti-establishment attitude. In response, he pulled out his helmet from Vietnam—one pocked with a bullet hole in it.

Harold made a convincing case for righteous revolution, but in the meantime, despite the drugs and drug-dealing, I was getting a master's degree. And earning straight As. This dual lifestyle rolled along, a grad student and his pretty wife in hazy bliss. In December 1970, our world got a jolt when Janet told me I was going to be a father. This time the news was joyous, if not scary. I had fathered a baby but not had the responsibility for one. How good a dad would I be?

And how strange was it one night during Janet's pregnancy when the phone rang, somewhat unexpectedly? We were almost asleep. I rolled over and grabbed the receiver and said "hello." When the response came, I recognized Tanya's voice instantly. "I wanted to let you know that you have a son," she said. I hadn't had any contact with her since she left New York three years ago. She somehow found out I was back in Muncie. But she hadn't found out other things. "I am married," I told her, "and we're having a child."

I didn't hear another word about her until twenty years later when her son—my son Michael—came to find me in New York City.

I wasn't around when Michael was born. For Lara's birth, I was in the waiting room at Ball Memorial Hospital—that's where expectant fathers were parked at the time. Lara was so beautiful.

The next day, I handed out pink joints at the office.

# CHAPTER 7
# Michigan

ANOTHER EXAMPLE OF MUNCIE'S WEIRD sort of proto-hipness lived a couple of doors away from us. They were an older lesbian couple, named Judy and Betty, one a professor at Ball State, the other a nurse. They were great neighbors, and when Lara was born they became instant godmothers. As a kind of parental subset, they would to talk to us about the future. One day they told us that they had some friends up in Michigan looking for a counselor at a middle school in Trenton, just south of Ford's massive River Rouge plant. "You should take the job," one of the women said. "You'd be perfect for it."

The interview process for Monguagon Middle School was cursory. School systems in the Detroit area needed people like me, and I was a freshly minted M.A. with an endorsement from respected professionals. Lara was one month old, cute and quiet in the back of the car as we crossed into Michigan. We rented a small house in Milan, about ten miles south of Ann Arbor. It was a tiny town set up on the side of a railroad track, but once we were there we decided that we wanted to live close to Ann Arbor, a college town that reminded us of Muncie, only cooler. Downriver Detroit, where I worked, was a thirty-minute commute.

But Milan didn't work for either of us. Janet may have been experiencing some postpartum depression, but mostly she missed Ball State, where we knew everyone. I sympathized. We were neither here nor there in Milan. My only relief came in the joints I smoked every morning as I drove our VW minibus to school.

After six months, we moved to Trenton, where I worked. Ann Arbor, a college town, would have been ideal, but it was too far away from school. Trenton was a car town. The auto industry had not yet collapsed at this point, but it was on its way. The children of those autoworkers populated Monguagon Middle School. Working with these kids as guidance counselor was rewarding, far better than teaching phys ed classes. They needed help fitting in, grappling with the usual adolescent insecurities, negotiating freedoms with parents, or learning how to focus academically.

But being out of the gym had its consequences. As in Muncie, my habit of smoking pot and munching doughnuts did not subside. I was a two-hundred-pound tub. Desperate for some physical outlet, I went to the administrators at the local high school and asked if I could work with some of the sports teams. They hired me immediately as the freshmen wrestling coach and varsity assistant. I started running and wrestled with the kids. The weight began to drop, five, ten, and then thirty-plus pounds.

What didn't drop was my drug use. It was what young teachers of that time did. Whereas once it was cool for students to sneak cigarettes, we were doing them one better. We'd gather behind the building and smoke pot. We weren't revolutionaries at that point, merely young people experimenting with brain chemistry. LSD and mescaline were beginning to make their way from campus to Detroit factory workers.

In a weird way, drugs meant community. Shortly after arriving in Michigan, I met a man named Steve, who worked as a substitute teacher. Steve and his wife became good friends of ours, and neighbors as well. When the upstairs apartment in our house became available, they moved in. Together, we smoked pot constantly and dropped a little acid. We'd go out for Baskin-Robbins ice cream, where trying to pick a flavor got ever more interesting.

Elizabeth Park was the first county park in Michigan and an oasis of peace, quiet, and even beauty at the end of my otherwise hardscrabble street. It was a place where I would run and, when I was done running, I'd sit on a bench to smoke a cigarette or a joint, look up at the sky, and strike up conversations with the other guys who were sitting and smoking. (It still hadn't dawned on me that smoking and running might be mutually exclusive exercises.) One of those guys was Ted, a short Polish guy with jet-black hair and a round face. Who knows how we struck up a conversation, but at some point we were talking about drugs. I must have mentioned LSD, and his ears perked up. He was curious. "You'll be out here again?" I said, and he nodded. "Okay," I said.

I'm all about sharing. After giving Ted a tab of acid, and then another, he became a convert. At the Ford plant where he worked, fighting the drudgery of assembly line duties was a daily battle, and LSD could help win that war. He had a customer base, he told me. And I had a supplier. I called Harold. The deal was this: I paid 23 cents per hit, and Ted bought them from me for $1 each. He could sell them for whatever markup he could get. The math worked quickly enough that I was moving thousands of tabs a month of Harold's trademark Mr. Natural acid.

Throughout the country, people caught with small amounts of controlled substances were doing hard time, but dealing didn't scare me for some reason. There were paranoid moments if shipments were late, but mostly I behaved as if we were dealing in mail-order fruit. And the fruit of my labor was producing an extra $500 to $1,000 a month. As an act of loyalty, I traded away my Volkswagen minibus and I bought a Ford van; although I'm not sure I'd have wanted those acid-dappled factory workers to assemble it.

This arrangement was slightly complicated by the fact that my landlord was a nice enough guy name Bob, who also happened to be a cop. More than once, Bob descended into the basement to fix the boiler or inspect a leaky pipe. That was, of course, where I stored my drugs and cash. Fortunately, he never discovered that his tenant was dealing.

In the 1960s, LSD had some proponents, including Harvard University psychology professor Timothy Leary, who lauded its mind-expanding properties. Decades later, Steve Jobs would suggest that LSD was a critical ingredient in expanding his own thinking. I certainly had a curiosity about how the brain and mind worked, and how to try to use it to maximum effect.

That led me to another out-of-the-box thinker, Jose Silva. Originally a radio engineer and technician in Texas, Silva had served in the Signal Corps during World War II. He became interested in psychology after undergoing a routine exam by a military psychiatrist, and over the course of a few decades he devised a set of self-help techniques to assist people in maximizing their brain power. He even claimed you could be clairvoyant. It was called Silva Mind Control, and it was taught at community centers and schools across the country. Although his techniques have been subsequently criticized by mainstream psychology, they remain somewhat popular.

Steve and his wife were the first adapters and they brought Janet and me into it. Silva Mind Control was a combination of the ordinary—meditation, visualization, clear thinking—with the added attraction of removing "negative energy." Ridding myself of negative thoughts entailed using a code phrase: "cancel/cancel." I had just been through two years of learning how to counsel kids, but I integrated some of the Silva techniques into my daily job. In fact, I still find some of Silva useful. Clearly, there's nothing terrible about trying to help a soccer player get rid of the negative energy in his head if he's had a bad first half.

Mind Control, naturally, got me thinking more broadly about mind and spirit expansion. Next on my voyage of spiritual discovery was astral projection. This was a process of using the power of your mind to leave your body and travel without it; for me I remember flying out over the Detroit River. I swear, there were no drugs involved.

Inevitably, I caught up with Timothy Leary and his associate Ram Dass, who believed in using LSD to unlock the doors of perception.

Dass was a trip in himself. Born Richard Alpert into a prominent Jewish family in Boston, he became a psychologist at Harvard and was soon a friend and colleague of Leary's. They started the Harvard Psilocybin Project, psilocybin being a natural hallucinogen found in certain mushrooms, and legal at the time. They gave it to volunteers and recorded their descriptions of the experience. The pair's lack of proper methodology would get them booted from Harvard, but they explored the outer edges of consciousness.

In the late sixties, Alpert transitioned to Baba Ram Dass, and in 1971, he wrote *Be Here Now*, a book that was hugely influential to me. Through Dass, I got to know a wide range of spiritual practices: Guru Kripa (devotional yoga focused on the Hindu spiritual figure Hanuman); meditation in the Theravada, Mahayana Tibetan, and Zen Buddhist schools; karma yoga; Sufi; and even Jewish mysticism.

This was, I admit, my own personal magical mystery tour— enlightenment and better living through drugs. But it was also about control. Harold had taught me to take control of my life by stealing credit card numbers and dealing drugs; those guys taught me how to take control of my surroundings. Some of those things seem silly from a distance, but they were very powerful at the time.

Despite these ventures into the far side of my mind, our lives had become somewhat settled after year one in Detroit. But come summer, there was only one way to go: back to Long Beach. I used to joke with Steve that the top two qualities of teaching were July and August. The first summer back in Long Beach, Lara learned to walk and we learned to stumble, partying from dawn until dusk, taking LSD, meeting my childhood friends. The Long Island crew seemed to be living their parents' lifestyle: in suburban houses with driveways and lawns. I probably felt a little bit smug about it when we left and got back to our lives in Detroit.

The second year at school was even better. I was no longer a rookie and I was finding success as a coach. Our varsity wrestling squad was one of the best in the state, and my freshman squad went undefeated. We had a visitor that year, my friend Ted, who was also a wrestler and a fraternity brother from Long Island. Ted—between jobs—crashed with us for a few months, in our spare room. Ted was a naturalist, and he'd go with me on walks in Elizabeth Park to identify all the birds and plants.

He also helped me coach wrestling and did drugs with me. I was a counselor at the middle school and a coach at the high school, so every afternoon I'd run home, nibble a small piece of acid with Ted, and head to wrestling practice. The acid gave me an edge to stay focused, which had to be dulled at night with Valium.

After all, that was life in the Motor City.

# CHAPTER 8

# New Mexico

I'M NOT EXACTLY SURE WHY the urge hit me again. In Nanuet, Janet and I made up our minds after a year that we couldn't abide a sedentary lifestyle, drugs or not. But we had made it to our third year in Detroit and something on the verge of normalcy was setting in. It wouldn't last. Silva Mind Control has no answer for that panicky feeling when you wake up and say to yourself: "I can't spend the rest of my life in Downriver Detroit."

In fact, I couldn't spend the rest of the year there. After the school year ended, I worked—with the assistance of a friend—on the inside of my van, building benches that could serve as beds and installing extra luggage racks. On a Saturday morning, Janet, Lara, and our dog Che (yes—Che, a German Shephard named after Che Guevera) loaded into the renovated Ford and began our next adventure.

Once again, we lacked a compass, but Janet and I knew where we had been: the Northeast, California, and of course the great Midwest. So something in our minds pointed south and west.

After about a week, we ended up in Aspen, Colorado. Today, Aspen is a Rocky Mountain Hollywood filled with the rich, famous, and overpriced, but Aspen in 1974 was still groovy: a hippie nation with young people, yogurt shops, health food stores, John Denver, and nonstop wiffle ball, the activity of choice. One thing hasn't changed: everyone was doing drugs. Pot is legal now, but not then.

We maintained Aspen as a home base, while also weaving in some camping time, and explored the area for its employment and living potential. Grand Junction, Colorado's western gateway, is north of Aspen and west of Vail, and it seemed more down-to-earth and friendly. Kingman, Arizona, which offered me a job on the spot, was the anti-Aspen, a lot more Wild West, and loaded with cowboys and rednecks, as much as there is a difference. I eventually reached the Navajo Nation in Gallup, New Mexico. The Navajo Nation had offered me the job also without even seeing me—that's how impressive my resume was. My aggrandizement shrank when I drove into the Navajo Nation in Gallup and saw that it consisted of eight trailers lined up along one side of the road. The desolation could suck the soul out of you. I'm sure those kids deserved a decent teacher, but it just wasn't going to be me.

We kept driving and stopped in Santa Fe, New Mexico. A couple of things happened. First and foremost, I was dazzled by the beauty of the place, tucked in as it was against mountains, yet colored in a desert palette. When I spotted an ad in the paper for a job at Santa Fe High School, I knew I had to apply. At least two hundred other teachers must have felt the same thing I did, as I found out when I submitted my resume.

We were staying at Black Canyon campground, on the road that goes to Ski Santa Fe in the Sante Fe National Forest. I drove deeper into the mountains to get some space to visualize the interview. Visualization was a Silva Mind Control technique, but it's also popular in sports psychology these days. The idea that kept coming to me was: "Go let him talk." To me, it was a signal that when I met the principal, Joe Casados, the interview should be about him, not me. A job interview is not always about you. And in this case, it was all about Joe. I told him how much I loved his ideas. And I'm sure I believed some of that.

The next day we were treated to a triple rainbow in the sky—could there be a better omen? When Casados offered me the job a week later,

I signed the contract and immediately hauled ass back to Trenton. We cleared out as quickly as possible, leaving most of our possessions on the front porch. We hadn't found a home in Santa Fe, so we pitched up in another campground when we returned, which was entirely pleasant in the fall.

It became clear pretty quickly that we had reached our new home. On the professional front, I was really excelling, due in part to the fact that the guy who had held the job before me at Santa Fe gave incompetency a bad name. And what a campus I got to call my "office;" it was more than two hundred acres. The kids were primarily Hispanic mixed in with Anglos and some Native Americans.

On the personal front, we found a place to live on Canyon Road, on the East Side of Santa Fe. There we met the perfect neighbors, the Alvarezes, whose family lived in New Mexico for hundreds of years, and who gifted us a spare refrigerator. Canyon Road felt like home instantly.

Unfortunately (though I may not have deemed it so unfortunate at the time), my drug life from Downriver made the move with me. That was somewhat of an economic necessity, given that the pay was lousy in New Mexico—I took a big pay cut. But I had a nest egg from dealing, $10,000 plus. I spent some of it on new wheels—a Nissan Patrol, the forerunner of the Land Cruiser and the kind of four-wheel drive beast needed for New Mexico's often-unpaved roads.

Given how much I loved the land here, I bought some. Driving around in my Patrol, I happened on available land near La Cueva, backing on the Jemez Mountains and a national forest. A thousand bucks an acre. I told Harold, too, knowing he needed to do some money laundering. La Cueva was forty minutes away from Santa Fe, the city was growing out, and one day the land would be developable.

The first week of my second year at the high school, I met a kid whose family owned some land closer to Santa Fe than the land that Harold and I had bought. It was seven acres or so, they said, in a village called Cañada de Los Alamos. I drove out to see it, and I was blown away. It was unbelievably beautiful, perched on the back of a mountain. I started talking to the couple, and they offered me the property for $25,000. By this time, I had started some light dealing again, pot and acid mostly, and I decided to pour all my money in the new deal. I called Harold and asked him to buy me out of the La Cueva property, which he did. I signed the papers and suddenly I was a landowner right there in Cañada de Los Alamos: five and a half acres just off the Old Santa Fe Trail.

That was to become my home, and more than my home. We moved in at the beginning of 1975, living in a trailer at first while we thought about what kind of dream house we wanted. Around that time, Janet got pregnant again. Lara had been planned. The second, Serene, was somewhat less planned. She was born in the trailer with the help of a homeopathic MD named Dr. Moscowitz. Afterwards, the doctor told me to hold out my hand. I thought he was going to shake it. Instead, he gave me crystals that turned out to be a kind of organic THC. Despite that, we were cleaning up a bit, or getting older, or both. Janet stopped using drugs entirely for a little while when she was pregnant and just after she gave birth.

Santa Fe rekindled my love for soccer, too. I discovered a pickup game at a small college called St. John's and played whenever I could. In the mountain air, what could be better? My game matured, too, and the more I played the stronger my legs got. There's no better drug on the planet than a soccer ball and some open space.

That's probably why I decided I had to share it. SFHS had loads of kids who played soccer—I'd see them all the time—but no formal team. In 1975, the Northern New Mexico Soccer League talked to me about founding a team at my high school. There wasn't enough budget money support for a varsity squad, but I got a club soccer team together and began to coach them and look for games.

Eventually, Santa Fe Prep agreed to play us. They were the big dogs in town. What Santa Fe Prep didn't know was that I had a secret weapon. By chance, I had run into a seventeen-year-old with the most ordinary name of Bruce Smith. Bruce attended another high school in town, but he in fact had grown up in Bolivia, where his father was a missionary. Bruce was better than anyone at either school. All I had to do once Bruce was signed up was assemble the rest of the parts: a good keeper, some decent defenders in front of him, and a couple of midfielders who could get the ball to Bruce's feet. He could do the rest. I drilled them like a college team for weeks.

In a manner similar to my attitude going into a big game today, I had a case of nerves on the day of the big game. Like today, it was more about excitement than doubt. If your team is prepared, you've done all you can do. The local newspaper even turned up to watch the newcomers take on the local dynasty. Bruce played like a big-game player, carrying the team on his back. We gave up a couple of goals, but Bruce knocked in two and we beat Prep by a 3–2 score.

The win gave impetus to a growing program. Soccer is a perfect sport in that it has absolutely no size limitations. Parents loved it and wanted their kids on my club team. As a coach, I wanted a varsity team; we had the ingredients, beginning with talent.

The time was right, too. Across the US, particularly in the suburbs, soccer was beginning to rise from its immigrant roots. This inevitably created conflict and competition with that other football, the one that oversized Americans play. When I approached our athletic director, a guy named Clyde Faucett, with the idea of starting a varsity soccer team, he looked at me as though I had asked to start the Junior Communist Club.

"Never," he said. He didn't even blink. Faucett was owned by the football families, the traditionalists. Soccer was a game they played in Europe and Latin America, wasn't it? They had little to fear at the time—American football wasn't going to lose any popularity because of us, but maybe Faucett was rankled because I was getting some publicity. Even then, I knew how to work the media.

I tried to reason with him. "I have a petition from parents," I said. "And the newspaper . . . "

He tried to shut me up. "We're not going to put it in," he said, and started to walk away. Wrong. I got stuck in, as the British say, and followed him, making my case as he tried to make his escape. He turned angrily toward me and push soon came to punch—I think we skipped the shove part. Two faculty members having a fistfight is not the most dignified exercise in education, but I wasn't backing down. Another teacher intervened to break us apart and I went home assuming that I would be canned. As it turned out, Principal Casados had my back, and the incident receded. There was a great lesson for me, though: the politics of local athletics really matter. You can do whatever you want with the curriculum, but mess with sports, and those are fighting words.

The other thing about soccer in America that Faucett may have miscalculated is the demographic that it attracts: upper-income families. My team attracted the rich white kids, and their parents were soon down Faucett's throat demanding varsity status. At the same time, the Northern New Mexico League petitioned to include us. We became a sanctioned varsity sport in 1978 and the first public high school team in the state of New Mexico. A year later, we were joined by Los Alamos High School, and the league started to really expand.

There was no stopping soccer's growth in New Mexico—or Texas and Arizona, for that matter. It spread to local public schools, which rushed to create programs so they could join our league. On the recreational level, I got an adult league going with lots of the area's working professionals: judges, lawyers, and accountants who had played the game before they moved to New Mexico. I also got a kids' league going and then a co-ed league. I was the Pied Piper of soccer. Things were going so well.

I was oblivious to the catastrophe looming down the road.

# CHAPTER 9
# Divorce

FOR MY THIRTIETH BIRTHDAY IN 1976—the year the United States turned two hundred—I figured a big bash was in order. And I had the perfect place to hold one, in Cañada de Los Alamos, with all that land. My birthday was in May, a perfect pretense for celebrating the end of school term, summer's start, and my arrival as a player in the Sante Fe scene. The guest list quickly got into the hundreds, including people from school, from soccer, and from the community. The plan was to have a frat party for grownups, complete with kegs of beer, all-night volleyball games, and whatever drugs came around. I swear I could have been elected mayor.

But I was losing one critical constituent. Janet was withdrawing a bit from me and even from Lara. I was initially clueless, but at one point I noticed that she was engrossed in a book, Gail Sheehy's *Passages: Predictable Crises of Adult Life*. It was a book about life stages that, from my perspective, turned her head around completely. It was at this point that she seemed to start to think about her life, which she had, until now, made subservient to mine and the kids'.

I had a full plate, from school to soccer to drugs to parenting to building a new house among these gorgeous mountains. It never occurred to me to think about how I was or wasn't meeting Janet's needs. One day we decided to take a family trip down to the historic

White Sands Missile Range. We suddenly became dysfunctional. Janet was horrible to me—and started to treat Lara badly. She sat in the back with Serene and left me and Lara in front.

What had I done? Why were we suddenly not communicating?

Though I couldn't reach her, she had a circle of friends, and I assumed that she was talking to them about her doubts and fears. One of her friends was a guy named Joey, a neighbor of ours. At one point during this cold front, Janet told me that she was going out for a hike with Joey. That seemed fine to me. But when she was gone for hours and hours, I started to worry. That night, when she came back, I sat down with her. "You're seeing someone else," I said.

She admitted she was having an affair with Joey. She told me she no longer wanted to be with me and was leaving.

We certainly weren't the first couple to be disrupted by a wandering spouse, although I'll admit I never for a second thought I would be the one who was cheated on. It was humiliating. I could only really share my plight with Ron, our former house guest now working at Santa Fe High as a math teacher, who had an inside view of our marriage. Ron urged me not to give up on Janet, which seemed reasonable enough.

At least it was until I met JoAnne, a buxom social worker who had been assigned to my high school. Janet was still in the house, but we were sleeping in separate rooms. JoAnne and I started seeing each other and it became clear to me that Janet and I were done. I told her about JoAnne, and before long Janet was gone. She moved to another house in town that I had bought with drug money. Initially she took both kids with her, but before long Lara came back.

A month later, JoAnne moved in, cuing the start of family dysfunction. How did we go from being a family unit to crazy?

Like a lot of jilted spouses, I suppose, perhaps I was trying to reconstruct my former life with a new wife. After JoAnne got pregnant about ten months into our relationship, we went to Canyon Road Park and had a quick hippie marriage.

But JoAnne was no hippie. In fact, she was straighter than a desert highway. Maybe that's why I was attracted to her, in some twisted way. Whereas Janet and I had been partners in crime for all our drug adventures, JoAnne was the anti-Janet. But I was still me. Worse, she would lecture me about my drug use, which only made me increase my drug use.

That included a drug called Chasing the Dragon. You take synthetic heroin, which is a white powder, and put it on tinfoil. You heat it up with a cigarette lighter, then inhale the smoke with a straw. This drug was different than the hashish, marijuana, cocaine, and the occasional Quaalude that I was doing. There was withdrawal, physical discomfort, and severe insomnia for a number of days with this new one. That was a message. I wished I had heard it.

What I didn't know initially about JoAnne is that she was well off and that became another poor reason to think we had a relationship. Her stepfather, a chemical engineer, lived with her mother on a hundred-acre ranch in Santa Barbara, California. Like her siblings, JoAnne had a trust fund of $100,000 worth of stocks. After one trip to see her parents, I convinced her to diversify: to use some of that money to help improve the Cañada de Los Alamos property. We added a second story with a beautiful master bedroom that overlooked the mountains. We also added a guest house. A fairytale mini estate!

Except, of course, for the people living under the roof. I still lived with the anti-Janet and she was about to have our child. She thought she lived with a worthless pothead, even though I continued to be well respected at work and in the community.

JoAnne's pregnancy was normal enough and when she went into labor, I summoned Dr. Moscowitz, the same naturopath who had delivered Serene. At one point I was downstairs when he was upstairs with JoAnne. I heard his voice and her voice as she went through the pangs of labor. Then everything ceased. Dr. Moscowitz shouted down to me, and I raced up the stairs. He greeted me at the top. There was no mistaking that something had gone terribly wrong. He explained to me that when the baby was being delivered, she swallowed her own meconium. She was dead. I had never seen a more beautiful baby in my life and now she was lifeless. We named her Amber Dawn, took her to the hospital, which confirmed the cause of death, and then we brought her home. We buried her in a coffin that a friend helped me build.

Our marriage was strained already, but losing a baby shattered it. JoAnne was inconsolable, and I returned to being uncontrollable. We finally came to the rational conclusion that we had to split. Just before that happened she got pregnant again. I was happy for her in a way, but I was not going to be there for her. She moved out and I moved on, behaving like a bachelor again, which is to say, irresponsibly.

But I did not neglect my children and they lived with me off and on, which was not all that difficult since Janet still lived in town. The kids and I liked to drive to Florida, where my sister and her husband Mike lived and ran a travel business. The kids played with Mike's daughter, and I partied with Mike and my sister, who shared my bad habits. On one of those trips, the conversation turned to Cañada de Los Alamos, and specifically the house expansion. Then, I invited them to live there.

And so they did: my sister, Mike, Michele their daughter, and their Irish setter. I loved my sister, and I was happy to have her there, but her arrival coincided with one of the heaviest drug phases in my entire time in New Mexico. Mike was from Peru—say no more. With the two of them living right next door, I had built-in babysitting and built-in partying.

And I needed the babysitting because Lara moved back, this time for good; her sister Serene stayed with Janet. She was then nine or ten years old, and becoming aware of the women, if not the drugs in my life. I was hardly a role model, but I tried my best to be a decent father. That summer, I struck up a relationship with a woman in town, Lisa, who was a prominent photographer. She mentioned the Lama

Foundation up in Taos, which was Ram Dass's place. During the summer, he would take kids and put them in yurts or huts or some kind of structure, and run a clown camp with Wavy Gravy, the famous hippie and peace activist. I enrolled Lara, and she seemed to thrive in it.

# CHAPTER 10
# Spiral

My birthday bash at the end of May had become an annual community blowout. We had everything that your average community gathering would offer—horseshoes, volleyball, and beer—plus a few things that are not normally on the menu, such as pot and Quaaludes. When you live on seven acres of land in pre–social media New Mexico, you could pretty much do what you wanted. We had fun celebrating my thirty-seventh birthday.

But this would be the last celebration, because I would soon meet a woman named Laura and a hurricane of drug addiction that would level me like island palm in what seemed like a heartbeat.

Despite the disruptions of two failed marriages and the death of an infant, my professional life hummed along. Soccer was always a great release for whatever domestic issue was troubling me and my job as a counselor was going along just as well.

Sometimes, on Friday night, I'd meet my sister and her husband at an Irish pub called the Green Onion. Quaaludes were my drugs of choice at the time, and kicking back with a couple of 'ludes and a margarita was an end-of-the-week ritual. One such Friday I spotted a beautiful black-haired woman at the bar. Laura had gorgeous big eyes and just stood out. I realized she was a switchboard operator at the school and recalled that she was recently divorced. She had a young daughter Lara's age, too. Sparks flew immediately.

Laura seemed to love me, but I was second to drugs. Our conversations dwelled on alcohol, Quaaludes, and marijuana, comparing combinations we liked. If JoAnne was draconian she was devilish, the anti-JoAnne.

Of course, I invited her to my birthday party. Things were rolling along like they usually did when Laura and I slipped into one of the bathrooms. There she took out this little yellow pill and a syringe. Curiosity had gotten me into trouble before back in Nanuet, when Ronnie had introduced me to skin-popping. Laura was about to raise the stakes. She tied my arm off and she shot me up.

Welcome to mainlining, Martin Jacobson. Welcome to the end of your life as it currently exists. The rush started at the base of my brain and went straight down my spine. This was Dilaudid, pure synthetic morphine. The high lasted an hour and a half, and then she shot me up again and that rush returned with ferociously great delivery.

Laura and her needle now comprised the center of my existence. The next day, she returned, and the day after. Other drugs had been playthings, toys that I could always put down and get back to work on Monday morning. Five days of Laura and Dilaudid, and I was hooked on both. I invited her to live with me and bring her daughter. As Shakespeare said it, "O judgment thou art fled to brutish beasts." The tragedy was about to ensue.

Dilaudid was the Oxycontin of its day, extremely powerful and subject to widespread abuse. Addicts quickly found doctors who would write prescriptions for anyone. Pill mills. Laura found Dr. Merrill Yordy in Española, about forty minutes from Santa Fe. She told me Dr. Yordy would write scripts for one hundred pills at a time. Dilaudid. The doctor was not one to question patients. He was there to help.

We drove to his office in Española. Laura went in for what seemed like thirty seconds and returned with a smile and a script. Dr. Feelgood was on the case. Sometimes, she would actually bruise herself so that she had a reason to ask for the drugs, although I'm not sure why she bothered. We'd take the script next door to Al's

Pharmacy. Were they in on the game? Who's to say? Who's to care? The high was that good.

There was a problem, though, which I recognized immediately. Withdrawal. Without Dilaudid, I got the shakes. You feel beyond horrible, and the only thing that will cure you is shooting up again. It's called a habit, and I am not being overly dramatic to say that within a week Dilaudid owned me. It had taken over my life entirely.

Which was manageable for a while. There we were, a happy little family of two nine-year-olds and two Dilaudid addicts. I still played soccer, I still worked at school. At the soccer field, I would wander off and get my fix behind a tree. At school, a stall in the teacher's bathroom was my shooting gallery. My kit went with me everywhere, a pharmaceutical security blanket. On the road, I shot up in the visitor's locker room. At a game in Roswell, New Mexico, I walked past the soccer pitch to the baseball field, slipped into the dugout, and shot up.

The Dilaudid even replaced the other loves of my drug life: Quaaludes, LSD, reefer. It replaced people, too, as I withdrew inside my life of Laura and Dilaudid. There was no room for anyone else. Tragically, I had money: maybe $10,000 in the bank. At a dollar a pill, a life of bliss seemed to beckon.

Then Dr. Bliss himself got busted, in February of 1984. Dr. Yordy was splashed across the paper, arrested for making too many people feel too good. Laura called me in a panic and we drove right out to Española. Dr. Yordy was down but not quite out of prescription pads. She scored a final batch of one hundred with Dr. Yordy, but our tolerance was at the point where a hundred pills could vanish within a week. Four days later we were strung out again, with nowhere to turn.

Desperate times call for more desperate measures. Laura knew her drugs—and that street heroin was the analog. We took the plunge. A guy named Viejo Joe took Dr. Yordy's place as our dealer. He was probably seventy, and he and his common-law wife Margie lived in the projects on the South Side of Santa Fe. He wouldn't sell to me, because

I was an Anglo; so Laura went in and came back out with the drugs. The heroin you could get in Santa Fe in those days wasn't very good, maybe only 2 to 10 percent pure. Didn't matter. I got buzzed and the nausea abated. We were paying twenty-five dollars a bag, and I was paying for her; my cost soared from five dollars a day in pills to two hundred or more in street drugs, which I could handle. Ironically, I had an account at Capital Bank, which had sponsored my adult soccer team. I was reminded of the cool Umbro uniforms the bank sponsorship had bought while I withdrew the money that was destined for the hole in my arm.

We had to ditch Viejo Joe because his goods were suspect and he was a sickly old man. We needed reliability and it appeared in the form of G, a six-foot-five half-Indian, half-Hispanic artist with tattoos all over his body. G had a rap sheet that included statutory rape and armed robbery. He had moved on to dealing and using. Laura went out to look for dope and G delivered: one bag for her and me, and he'd take one for himself.

Before long G owned me. Before him, I was a recreational drug abuser who could manage a job, a family, a variety of wives, ex-wives, and girlfriends, be a parent, and run a household. After him, a hard-core addict. My connection to Laura? Gone. She and her daughter moved out. Within a few years she would be dead from an overdose. But at that moment in time, there was me and G and heroin. He was a powerful man with persuasive powers and after a time he was controlling most of my ideas, or rather my wallet. My bank account became his: $200, $300 a pop. The guy who was a community leader in May was being led around by a lowlife that winter. He separated me from my friends. He bought me a gun, a .45. I practiced shooting. I slept with it.

For anyone who knew me at this time, the idea that I might become a criminal would have made them incredulous. This guy's a high school guidance director and popular coach at Santa Fe High School, on the South Side of town. People respected me, sought my advice. Parents would wave as they drove by. During the lunch hour I used to go to the health club and meet with Governor Jerry Apodaca for a racquetball game. Then I'd go back to work in my nice car.

A few years after befriending Jerry, his old racquetball partner would be scoring drugs in the nearby projects. He wouldn't have imagined "the coach" would now go to Viejo Joe's apartment, the Sangre de Cristo projects, to score.

This was a career path to hell. Arrive in New Mexico in 1974 for a new adventure; become a heroin user by 1982. There can be only one outcome here: crash. As a lot of people can attest to, you can spend $5 on your first high and $500,000 before you're either clean or dead. It's a path you never see coming. I already had a lot of experience as a drug user; I thought I could handle anything. For me the start was Dilaudid, that's the precursor to Oxycontin, which is ravaging our country today. When Dilaudid became unavailable, heroin then seems like a good alternative. As the saying goes, that's why they call it dope. Your life as an educator is now swallowed by your life as an addict. Your job now isn't to coach kids on the proper technique for heading a ball. Your job is to GET DRUGS NOW.

And so I did, until I had constructed a habit costing up to $1,000 a day. You don't fund that on a teacher's salary, obviously. But you can convert real estate to heroin fairly easily. One house after another was sold chasing score after score, until the score was heroin: everything, Jake: zero.

Living the life of a junkie is not without thrills. On a shopping trip to Margie and Joe's shooting gallery, I got into a tiff with another customer, a large lady named Modesta. We fought over a dope issue, naturally, and it was for that cause that Modesta felt compelled to grab a large kitchen knife and try to stab me to death. I blocked the blade with my hand and, bleeding profusely, grabbed a towel, wrapped my hand, and ran out of the apartment. If it had occurred to me that I could score some painkillers at the ER getting my hand stitched up, I might have gone there. Instead, I found another place to score.

Without lapsing into any stereotypes, it would be fair to say that for the most part I was the only white dude out among mostly Hispanic junkies who would make our way to another set of projects on the North Side of Santa Fe. And most dealers don't care; they will happily sell to people of all colors, sizes, and shapes. But one day, trying to enter the projects, I encountered this very strong, very crazed Hispanic guy who did not care for Anglos, as whites are called there, and especially didn't care for this Anglo. The angrier he got as we walked toward the building, the less concern I had for scoring, the more I did for living. The fight or flight impulse was fairly screaming: FLIGHT. So I took off until, figuring I was at a safe distance, I looked back. A slight miscalculation had been made. He'd pulled out a gun and was aiming it at me. Bang. The shot just about parted what hair I had left.

In soccer, there's something called a recovery run. If your team loses the ball in the opposing end, you've got to haul your ass back on defense for safety. This was the ultimate recovery run. And my last trip to that particular location.

My addiction would last until my assets ran out, a process that would take the better part of three years. That's usually the way it goes, isn't it? Unless you O.D. or commit a crime and get incarcerated. There were costs well beyond money. Lara's reaction to my condition was to act out herself. How else was a twelve-year-old going to get attention from her junkie father? Friends and family fell by the wayside; they would try to help, but how many times are they going to be lied to before they stop having anything to do with you?

Then it's just you and your addiction, your selfishness. "You better get clean now," I must have told myself, "or you won't see the end of 1986." Having sold or lost most of my houses, and leaving my job at Santa Fe High, I liquidated my retirement fund—$60,000—and over ten weeks, my last ten in New Mexico, spent it as I had the last three years.

By the summer of 1985, I was going to work, but everyone there knew that something was wrong. If they said anything to me, I tuned them out. I was playing soccer, but my game went downhill rapidly and I gradually lost interest in the sport I loved the most. Whatever parenting I was doing could not have been useful.

In one of his songs, singer/songwriter Neil Young compares junkies to a setting sun.

And now I was slipping below the horizon.

# CHAPTER 11

# The Prodigal Son Returns

IF YOU HAD YOUR CHOICE of getaway cars, you would probably not select a beat-up, ten-year-old Subaru as the most expeditious means to exit a crime scene. Neither would I. But then again, I never anticipated that I would be the getaway driver in an armed robbery.

Then again, when you are a junkie, your judgment is, shall we say, compromised. On this particular day, G had me drive him to a pharmacy in downtown Santa Fe, a store named Free Frasier Pharmacy, which was just off the Paseo de Peralta—a street that runs across and around the state capital.

My 1980 Subaru station wagon was going through the throes of death and so, you could say, was its owner. G told me to wait for him while he went inside to transact business. A couple of minutes later he came out running. He had a gun in his hand, apparently having misplaced his credit card. Not really. "Let's get out of here," he yelled. He was carrying what looked like a regular grocery bag, but he had not gone in there to go shopping for vitamins.

He'd cleaned out the pharmacy. I think the pharmacist's name was Joe. G and his hardware had quickly persuaded the terrified Joe to open the safe—a treasure trove of pharmaceutical cocaine, Dialudid, codeine, Percodan, and every controlled substance under the sun. We drove out of town on a dirt road back to Canada, where I still had a house, or what was left of one. We were exhilarated, shocked, scared, drug-hungry, and paranoid.

My house was like a trailer park after a tornado had come through it. That was an apt metaphor for my life, too. I'd stripped the house of pretty much all the furniture—anything I could sell. There was a mattress and some guns. We set up the mattress against the window of the upstairs balcony. We could see down the long driveway and in our paranoid state we believed that there'd actually be a shootout with the cops. For reasons unknown to me, nothing happened.

Then we began taking the drugs, moving between paranoid alertness and hallucination. We stayed in that room for days and worked through that grocery bag full of drugs, one of us with a rifle in his hand, the other holding a .45.

How remarkably lucky for me that the cops didn't catch up with us, weren't interested, or had something more urgent to do. We could have been gunned down, and rightly so.

Four months later, I made up my mind to leave New Mexico. That decision saved not only my life, I like to think that it would eventually save other lives too.

This was a terribly difficult choice for me. Santa Fe, New Mexico, was a town where I might have spent my entire career. I loved the community, the kids, the mountains, my children, a couple of women—but mostly I loved heroin. That is never a good relationship to have and the most difficult to break off. Before we parted company, heroin had claimed my houses, my 401k, my friendships, and my job. It could have claimed my life at any given moment.

I had to leave this beautiful place to save my ugly life. And I got a little push, too. The state police had closed in on my burgeoning (if not bungling) career in crime. It would only be a matter of time before the craving would put me in a position to feed it via some crime or another and the cops were already waiting for it to happen. One aspect of policing I would come to understand is that the cops aren't always looking to bust you. They'd be just as happy if you became someone else's problem in some other jurisdiction.

That's why they offered me the choice of getting out of town or getting arrested. Guess what I chose?

At least this would be a legal getaway—with money I got from ratting out a friend to the cops (well, there really are no friends among junkies, but I think you get my drift). And so it was that I bought two tickets to New York on People's Express airlines, one of the early low-budget carriers and one of the worst, as it's long gone.

There are some figures or statistics that you never forget, and this is mine: $1.23. That was the sum total of the money in my pocket when I arrived at Newark International Airport.

Here I was, daughter Lara in hand, and financially, emotionally, and spiritually broke. It made me understand how resilient kids can be in the face of adversity. Maybe I sensed it then, too. I always tried to be a good father to Lara, but how good a father can you really be when heroin is the head of the household? She'd seen me cry, tremble, and run. And running we were—me from a very ticked-off drug dealer who would have loved the option of shooting me, and Lara from the madness I had poured into her young life as I did the poison in my veins.

So it was that we returned to where the story began, in Long Beach, New York, where I grew up. My mother, who had endured her son's implosion from a sad distance, now had it in her face. But not for long. She took us in for a couple of days and made sure I knew this was a stopover, not a destination. It was more than I deserved, to be honest. So, we moved on quickly. Another friend offered a couple weeks of shelter, which we gladly accepted.

I was not a stranger in Long Beach. Like many New York City Jews, we moved from congested Brooklyn to what then seemed like a distant suburb when I was three years old. Long Beach is another world from Brooklyn, a beautiful beach town thirty-five miles from midtown

Manhattan that could pass for a suburb of LA. My mother's home has now become my summer home and a four-season sanctuary. As with any place, there are good and bad times: my father withered and died here. His chronic illness and deterioration weighed heavily on me; I learned to play soccer, as a form of therapy. Little did I know, soccer would loom as a therapy again in a few years.

Familiarity allowed me the credibility to borrow some money from old buddies—they must have been horrified at what they were looking at. They remembered the soccer and wrestling star they thought would go far on his gifted feet. I did, just not in the direction they anticipated. But they never lectured; they just hoped for the best. With enough cash to rent a place for half a month, I got Lara back into 9th grade. To earn enough money for the full month's rent, I started driving a hack. Which could be viewed as ironic, I suppose, or just sad. Because after my father's own business fell apart because of his medical issues, he started to drive a cab to help support us.

Now here I was in the same position, albeit for different reasons. That didn't matter though. The ocean air filled my lungs with the fresh smell of a new beginning. We took a basement apartment on Mitchell Avenue for $250 a month. That sum afforded us a living room, kitchen, and bathroom. Among the people who helped was my old friend, Tommy—a cop who has seen the dark side of addiction from a professional perspective. He'd give me some money and probably figured it's 50/50 that it would end up in my arm. Two Catholic nuns also helped out, demonstrating their vow of charity by giving a Jewish boy some help and a mattress for Lara to sleep. The floor would do for me. An apt metaphor. How great is it to have a floor under you?

Lara learned to navigate this distorted world that I created. She accompanied me to the meetings, listened as I said that my name is Martin, that I'm an alcoholic. As if she didn't know. You expected her to say, "you haven't heard half of it." She'd been a witness to my destruction, watched me withdraw before. Too many times she'd had to see the physical toll taken on a body still in addiction's clutches, every bone hurting, fighting the urge to want to rip my own skin out. If anything, she understands human failure. And I swore that I would strain until I became a hero to her again.

Christmas quickly approached, and I was hardly in a position to play Santa Claus. Not after a couple of personal bankruptcies and notwithstanding the fact that I'm, technically speaking, Jewish. But I longed to do something for Lara, who was raised ecumenically. The holiday spirit that infused my customers trickled down to me. I'd gotten about $150 in the piggy bank by mid-December, a sum that would have been insignificant to me when I was dealing drugs.

For the time being, we were reliving the redemption that Jimmy Stewart experiences in *It's a Wonderful Life*. For us, that meant going to buy a Christmas tree—a little five-dollar tree that was scrawny by any measure but, symbolically, a redwood. We were standing straight and tall and the optimism I was feeling wasn't some kind of seasonal sensory overload. Remorse and then relief at being back home gradually hardened into resolve.

I am, after all, a competitor. Even as a drug dealer, I was good and resourceful. Never one for flash, all the money I earned dealing drugs went into real estate, a fairly conservative asset play. Before my own roof caved in, I owned five homes in New Mexico, including one on 7.2 acres of land on the old Santa Fe Trail in the village of Cañada de Los Alamos. We were nestled at the foothills of the Sangre de Cristo Mountains, just outside Santa Fe. It was the definition of the American Dream, somewhat inconveniently financed by a scheme and a citizen above suspicion.

One of the problems with quitting drugs cold turkey is that feeling that you can't sit still. This is a particular problem if you are driving a cab for a living. Given my parlous economic situation, I was driving the overnight shift, six in the evening until six the next morning, and taking on as much overtime as I could manage. Of course, there were no benefits and healthcare, unless you call AA a medical plan.

Withdrawal is not a one-day or one-week or one-month experi-ence. It is riding on an ocean of pain, one with unforeseen swells that knock you for a loop. Every bone in my body hurt. I had this feeling, this all-day feeling of wanting to change my blood. I swear my blood hurt as it coursed through my veins. Think of your worst hangover, then magnify that by a thousand. You're getting close.

To manage this DIY withdrawal, I was relying on Clonadine, the low blood pressure drug that I rounded up back in New Mexico. I started taking it two weeks before I left New Mexico. One of its side effects left me tired and weak. And at the same time sleepless. And when you do manage to fall asleep, Clonidine delivers nightmares to your subconscious. I would dream about shooting up. I would have dreams that would scare me awake, leaving me shaking, weeping. If you wonder why junkies relapse, consider this: it takes a year before you feel normal again. Although it feels like five. By February I was trying to get off the crutch that was the Clonadine, trying to cut back to one or two a day to nurse me through the worst symptoms.

AA is famous for its twelve-step program. But I found that recov-ery is a million of them. Nevertheless, you keep going forward, one foot in front of the other, all day. Everyday. Driving the cab became a metronome of sorts from A to B to A to C. Accelerate, brake, try to make a conversation to alleviate the boredom. Sometimes after a shift, I came home to lie on the floor and had no memory of the last twelve hours. The pain and the tiredness owned me.

And you are faced with reminders of your worst self, the drunks and drug-addled getting in and out the back seat. Wouldn't it be great to feel like them for thirty seconds? No, it wouldn't. I was trying to remember where they said they wanted to go. Trying to remember where I needed to get to.

The company owned the cab. I had no car of my own and that bicycle was still a dream. I was walking everywhere in the New York winter. I wished I had a bike, but even without one I'd still got to attend meetings and get to my daughter's school, my feet tramping the streets I grew up on.

My mother remained supportive, hopeful. Wary. But she was looking out for her boy. She called me one day to point out an ad she saw in the *New York Times*. My mother was looking for a job for me. It's a job for a teacher, she said. The Joseph Lanzetta School, PS 96, in East Harlem, up at 120th Street between 2nd and 3rd avenues. This neighborhood used to be an Italian-American ghetto ("ghetto" is an Italian word) but the poor Italians have long been supplanted by poor blacks and Hispanics. In other words, it's a tough location—why else do they have to advertise? But this was also what I knew and loved.

I would like to say that I aced the interview, but the truth is that anyone with a teaching certificate and a pulse would have been offered the job. Even getting to PS 96 presented its share of speed bumps. At the corner of 116th and 1st, dealers were moving bags of heroin like they were street cart hot dogs. Passing that corner every day on the way to the bus stop for my ride home was unnerving at first. My pace quickened a little. My vision narrowed as I stared ahead unfocused. No eye contact. I was terrified that they'd know.

The greater challenge was in the classroom. This was a Special Education class for twelve- to fourteen-year-old emotionally disturbed boys. There was nothing special about it. These kids were here because the city didn't know what else to do with them. Nor did their teachers. I discovered that five teachers quit who held this position over the last couple of years. These kids probably figured I'm just going through the turnstile like the rest.

The kids were mostly crack babies. Crack is smokable cocaine, and in the late 1980s it unleashed an epidemic of addiction that absolutely overwhelmed the city's social and criminal justice systems. Crack was too cheap, amazingly addictive, and crackheads and crack dealers were capable of unfathomable violence under its influence. The murder rate skyrocketed to more than two thousand annually vs. 289 murders in 2018. Worse, the children of crackheads would suffer from serious debilitation.

Now these kids were mine. And I'd never taught anything academic before—just gym classes. Which is just as well, as the job amounted to little more than crowd control. Like their parents, they were prone to violence, and I had to break up fights every day. The kids were like me, damaged by drugs. We're all just walking into the classroom every day. They struggled with the terrible hand they'd been dealt through no fault of their own. I struggled with the idea of getting clean and weaning myself off the Clonidine—all of which was my fault. Dealing with these kids, who deserved so much more, still to this day weighs heavily on me.

Maybe this is how the gods were getting even with me for nearly throwing away my career as an educator. Here you go, Jacobson the junkie, you try to teach emotionally disturbed kids in East Harlem whose circuits were fried by their junkie parents. So they threw me, sweating, freezing, and lurching from withdrawal, into a room already filled with the aching needs of eleven of these kids. They're throwing chairs. They're tearing each other apart. Their teacher can't sleep, can't focus, and every day he walks past dope dealers who would send him back to hell.

It's a living. Ya know?

# CHAPTER 12
# Jailbird

IMAGINE YOUR WORST NIGHTMARE. GETTING fired publicly? Going broke? Being dumped by a lover or embarrassed by a badly advised Instagram post? Clearly, you're not trying.

When I was hired by the New York City public school system to deal with the absolutely most challenging children in the history of education I was extremely grateful and extremely diligent. At the very least, I did my best with the crack babies, now grown into wild children, in my charge. But on a ghastly hot day in June in 1986, my efforts would be rewarded by a visit from a couple of NYPD detectives. They were not there for show and tell.

Auggie Saccochio, the assistant principal of PS 96, knocked on the door of my classroom and told me he'd mind the class for a bit, because I was needed at the principal's office. I couldn't imagine what I was needed for until the two detectives, officer Lynch and officer Carter, asked who I was. My principal, Nydia, had no idea about my past life, but clearly the detectives did. When I told them, they said "Martin Jacobson, there is a warrant for your arrest in New Mexico."

Those crushing words ended a period of denial. When I'd applied for the job at PS 96, I'd submitted fingerprints like all other employees. In the still largely unconnected world of the time, those prints had been worming through the system until they matched up with the prints of a guy wanted in New Mexico. A guy named Martin Jacobson.

You ever get that sick-to-your-stomach feeling, as if you are falling from a great height and are scared blind? I stood in Nydia's office trying hard not to throw up, soil myself, or do both at the same time. I wanted to cry. I wanted to be anywhere else.

Things change so quickly. This day was like a microcosmic version of my old life. When I'd walked into Nydia's office I was a teacher and everyone was nice and civil, but the relationship had shifted. I was a teacher when I was outside the door. I was a suspect when I crossed the threshold and confirmed who I was. I was not allowed to make a call right here. I was not allowed to just walk out into the afternoon sun.

A warrant! My head ran through the possibilities. There were many.

Worst scenario first. Armed robbery. I am replaying the movie in my head of the drug store robbery in which I unwittingly became the getaway car driver. So there was that possibility. Armed robbery and whatever they could throw in, starting with conspiracy and ending, I suppose, with receiving stolen goods—goods that were injected into my arm. That came with the possibility of being extradited and having to face a long stretch for it. And extradition, my mind was racing now, would bring me back into the orbit of a couple of those folks who just then wanted to kill me.

A strange kind of relief came with the information that the charges involved forgery and fraud—non-violent crimes. Just before I escaped New Mexico I'd been writing some checks that lacked an account from which to pay them. And payment, it appeared, was now due. They took me out, into the car, and to an office on Centre Street in downtown Manhattan. My hands were cuffed behind my back.

The detectives were good with me though. They were just two guys from the warrant division, and I was one of the least threatening criminals they'd have to deal with that day. If not for the cuffs, you might have thought I was one of them. First, they handcuffed me to a chair. Later they cuffed me with waist cuffs, shackles so tight that I could hardly move my hands in front of me. Then I was taken for mug shots.

When they had me in the office, they kept me there as long as possible so I could avoid Central Booking for as long as possible. Central Booking, I was given to understand, was the next circle of this hell. They even offered me a sandwich. I was too distraught, too anxious, to eat it, but later I would wish that I had. I wouldn't eat again for a few days.

When I got my phone call, I called Anne-Marie, my girlfriend at the time, who in turn got in touch with my mother for me. Despite all the disappointment I had piled on her, my mother got to work on getting me some legal help.

Eventually, the detectives could keep me sitting in front of them no longer. I was taken to a holding cell—although holding *hell* might be the better description. You may hear horrible things about jails in foreign countries, but I can tell you that America has just as big a claim on inhumane treatment as Russia or Thailand or anywhere else. In the pen, I was handcuffed to the guy next to me. There were four of us pushed into a four-foot-by-four-foot cage—there's no other word. This dehumanization is part of the process in which you are shipped from cell to cell, from hell to hell. By then you realize that all there is to eat and drink is baloney and Kool Aid.

I was a novelty. The only white guy anywhere to be seen among a group of black or Hispanic men, some of them cops or correction officers. The criminal justice system in some ways reflects the society around it. A century ago, a black guy would have stood out in a sea of Irish cops and criminals. Among the inmates, everyone else seemed like a bigger mess than me. It was a little bit scary, a little bit inspiring. This second cell I was moved to was larger, some sixteen feet by sixteen feet, but with twenty people packed into it. For our convenience, there was one toilet in the corner, a toilet that was sending out olfactory reminders of what is still the hottest day I can remember. Then the grip of fear was replaced again by the familiar grip of withdrawal.

The smell could make putrid feel like perfume. No wonder everyone was fighting over cigarettes—which seems odd in these smoke-free days, but cigarettes were hugely important among prisoners. Plus, a little smoke could at least change the olfactory score. All of us were handcuffed in the front with the waist cuff. I'd just arrived when I realized I had to pee. There's an art to pissing when your hands are in waist cuffs, one I learned when I stood dry retching over the dark crater of a toilet. For the life of me I couldn't get my zipper unzipped, as if I'd never taken a piss before. Although I never had had to take a piss with my hands chained together. When I finally figured it out, the relief was real.

Later, this light-skinned Hispanic guy got tossed in with us, and in an instant the whole place erupted into a fight over cigarettes. The new guy said something in Spanish to another guy and suddenly, bam bam. I remember the correction officer looking in at me, this white guy in khakis. The look on his face said, what the fuck are you doing in there? I sensed that he didn't want to know the back story.

This holding cell was in the middle of Central Booking. The wheels of justice were apparently grinding, papers were being pushed and they next escorted me to another area where I was paired up and pushed into this cave-like place, just two to a cell now. We were luxuriating in space, maybe eight feet by eight feet.

*Maybe the worst is over*, I was thinking. *This isn't so bad*. I was sharing with one guy. *I can deal with this cellmate business at this level. I can handle this.* He was a Hispanic guy, Julio. He was slight in build and presumably he had been disarmed. I wasn't too afraid.

But the machinery was moving, and soon, so was I. They took us now, all the doubles, and moved us to a new and scarier hell—a large 30 by 30 foot holding cell, the place crowded like a rush hour subway ride whose passengers are uncontrollably violent and on the verge of insanity. There was an impassive CO, his humanity having been drained by his dreadful occupation, always looking in and doing little. Arguments erupted all the time. Short of murder, I'm not sure what would have prompted him to intervene. Couldn't blame him, I suppose; it was much safer where he was.

The inmates would go after you for that cigarette that they imagined you were concealing. They would go after you for that look they imagined you shot at them. The guys in the cell called the correction officers COs as if it were one word, sea-oh. Hey sea-oh! My instinct, in contrast, was to address these COs as "Sir." Then again, my instinct was to address my cellmates as "Sir" also. There was a large fan blowing hot sweaty air into the cell, and a large window above that was open, blessing us with daylight for awhile.

All these rooms and questions and process, and I was still just into the night of a day that began in a classroom. I was still in the same clothes I had on at the moment Auggie knocked on the classroom door: a pair of light-colored khakis, sneakers, and a polo shirt. It was as if a Sears appliance salesman had turned up at a cage match.

There was a guy in the cell freaking out. At last, I had something in common with one of my cellmates: being a junkie. His symptoms were familiar. He couldn't get his methadone and he was hallucinating. I began keying on him to keep myself strong. Looking at the poor wretch, I could say to myself: I'm clean, at least I'm clean. The guy was in early withdrawal, screaming in incredible pain. Been there. Done that. At least three different times. Never again. Watching him suffer forced me to suck whatever courage I could from his plight.

In the New York system, they keep you riding on the carousel of justice until you get to court, which was a day and a half later. There is no New York minute in the court system. By that time nothing severe had happened to me. Just the fear of it. No stabbing. No buttfucking. No fighting. No eye contact. You learn quickly to keep to yourself. You develop your own little mantra. Plea bargaining with your personal god. *Just get me through this. Just get me through. I'll be good. I'll be clean. You listening?*

In the big cell, everyone eventually nodded off. I used my shoes as a pillow. I got maybe two or three hours in, sleeping, as the saying goes, with one eye open. You're shifting on the hard cement floor, sweating through the night, getting up to pee, stepping over inmates, scared that a careless footstep might trigger a riot. I inhaled the fetid aroma of other dirty bodies. There was a small sink but no towels, just toilet paper to dry off with. And no street noises at all, just the sound of snoring and breathing filling the vacuum. The air was still and stagnant and somehow always threatening.

I breathed that fetid air for the better part of another day. The outside world ceased to exist. Everyone is just waiting for his name to be called. Finding out how it all works was the hard part. I buddied up to a CO. Asked him what was going to happen. The answer was simple. You just wait and wait. Eventually something will happen.

I wouldn't eat during the entire time I was there. I kept staring at a spot on the wall. I was sweating. Monotony makes it the worst cell time you can imagine—it's not like you can get on your cellphone. Finally, you got a sort of spiritual high from the deprivation, the heat, the concentration, the hunger. I'm not saying it was a fun experience. It was the opposite. Just that it could have been worse. There was joy in surviving. What doesn't kill you makes you stronger sort of thing.

At around 4 p.m. my name was called—finally. For my poor mom, trying to find me in this system was its own Kafkaesque process. When they called my name, I was told that I would be moved outside. Nothing happens quickly though. Not in there. It would be around 7 p.m. by the time they rounded enough of us up.

The process. It just wears on you. Back to the light or away from it for a long time. The process carried me and my fellow prisoners in a paddy wagon next. Old style. To the Tombs, the infamous cells across from the court's chambers. Leg cuffs added for the journey. I wanted to reach the Tombs though. They'd rebuilt the place the year before, and it was now air-conditioned. It was, nonetheless, New York's most famous hellhole. It was the Shangri-La for me. Finally, I had something to eat, some horrible hamburger, but who cared?

Coach Jake in the early days with his mom, dad, and sister.
(*Photo courtesy of Martin Jacobson*)

Getting ready for the Final, circa 2005. L - Emelio Haughton C - Biko Edwards
R - Tetsu Yamada. (*Jason Gould, WWW.JASONGOULD.NET*)

MLK team being honored at City Hall with former mayor Michael Bloomberg (center, kneeling). (*Photo courtesy of Martin Jacobson*)

The MLK team poses for a 2007–08 championship photo.
(*Photo courtesy of Martin Jacobson*)

The MLK team poses for a 2016–17 championship photo.
(*Jason Gould, WWW.JASONGOULD.NET*)

A good warmup before a game. (*Jason Gould, WWW.JASONGOULD.NET*)

The 2016 team fought back in a massive double-overtime win to claim a championship.
(*Photo courtesy of Martin Jacobson*)

Coach Jake Raising the Cup . . . with the 2016 NYC champions.
Executive Director Donald Douglas of the Public School Athletic League looking on.
(*Jason Gould, WWW.JASONGOULD.NET*)

Team huddles beneath the Bridge at Randall's Island.
(*Jason Gould, WWW.JASONGOULD.NET*)

On the way to a semifinal game, the squad takes two trains and a bus
to Randall's Island. Coach Jake prepares the team for the journey.
(*Jason Gould, WWW.JASONGOULD.NET*)

The 2018 captain and All-American Yaya Bakayoko with volunteer assistant coach Shomari Ramsey. (*Jason Gould, WWW.JASONGOULD.NET*)

Centerback Eric Affi celebrates with center midfielder David Gomez alongside. (*Jason Gould, WWW.JASONGOULD.NET*)

Captains Rashawn Best and Yaya Bakayoko with the MLK starters in a team huddle before the championship game in 2018 at St. John's University.
(*Jason Gould, WWW.JASONGOULD.NET*)

Some of the MLK coaching staff with Coach Jake after winning another championship.
(*Photo courtesy of Martin Jacobson*)

During the 2018 Final, Coach Jake looks on with Associate Head Coach Josh Sherron. (*Jason Gould, WWW.JASONGOULD.NET*)

Coach Jake poses with former players at a 2018 Nike event. (*Photo courtesy of Martin Jacobson*)

I was coming through, but there would be one threat. It was in The Tombs that I encountered him—a tall, black, acne-pocked tough guy who had been charged with murder. Melvin wanted to have a push-up contest with me. Fine. I started doing push-ups in front of him so he wouldn't bother me. Manic push-ups. After this performance, he asked what I was in for. Bad checks was not going to cut it. Armed robbery, I told him. And murder. He didn't bother me after that. Murderous mutual respect, perhaps.

In the Tombs, I waited for the outcome of the lotto draw. We all had a pad to sleep on, plus a pillow and a blanket. The cell was cleaner. In the draw, I could get either a trip to court or a trip to Rikers Island to await a hearing. Part of my heart was sinking slowly. Rikers Island. Rikers Island. More infamous than the Tombs, and a lot less safe. Two words that spell "deep shit." A place so awful that the mayor of New York wants to close it.

Finally, they called my name. I was a winner; I would be going to my hearing, not to Rikers. By 11 a.m. they were transporting the rest of my fellow arrestees to Rikers. And me, the lotto winner, I'd get a ride back to the courthouse via the wagon and in chains.

At the holding cell outside the court, I encountered even more luck. My mother had hired a competent lawyer, who had been busy. He'd negotiated a deal between the district attorney in New York and his counterpart in New Mexico. They were able to agree, even though this was an extradition case, to allow bail on the condition that I return to New Mexico. Keeping me, now a responsible citizen, in jail didn't make sense to them, thankfully. Returning to New Mexico to face the charges at this point seemed like returning to paradise. The gears turned for another day before I was finally bailed.

It was dark out by the time of my release. I met my mother and Anne-Marie standing outside in the real world just through the big door. They had just met each other for the first time. I asked about Lara. She'd been staying with a friend in Long Beach. My world was intact. I thanked the women who had saved me, kissed them. I'd survived the ordeal.

The oddest thing is that I came out with this spiritual high from surviving and fasting. At least I was still clean. Yet questions remained. Would I have to go to jail in New Mexico? Would I end up driving a cab for the rest of my life? By this point, the Board of Education was involved. A convicted felon could never teach.

Somehow, though, I knew I'd never use again.

# CHAPTER 13
# Rebound

A WEIRD THING HAPPENED TO me recently when I applied for the Global Entry program, a program run by US Customs and Border Protection that makes life easier going through US Customs when you're traveling. My background check turned up an issue tied to charges in New Mexico in 1984 that had been long resolved. They denied my application. To think I was still a wanted fugitive three decades later! To get approved, I would have to appeal the decision and show the papers I received from the state of New Mexico dropping the charges of fraud for check kiting. And they still gave me a hard time.

Perhaps this was a reminder from the gods to keep my nose clean. But these same gods must have wanted me to have a second chance. How else do you explain my Jonah-like escape from the mouth of the New York City jails and the New Mexico penal code? Well, perhaps it was the gods and my mother. After all, she was the one who found a lawyer for me by walking around the criminal courthouse in lower Manhattan and interviewing attorneys until she found one who had a connection in New Mexico. She was a firebrand of a woman and she needed to deal with what I put her through.

When I was sprung from my three-day vacation in hell, it was under the condition stipulated by the DA in New Mexico that I would return there to surrender. There would be no extradition, meaning I wouldn't be escorted back to Santa Fe in handcuffs. Heck, just being an airline passenger is punishment enough.

The DA and my just-hired-by-Mom New York lawyer worked out a deal that I would return in early September. It was late in June and school was about to be recessed for the summer. Returning to school wouldn't be possible unless the charges were dropped or I was found innocent. Of course, if I was sentenced to New Mexico State Prison my teaching career might be interrupted forever.

That summer I went back to driving a cab and driving myself crazy thinking about what was to come. I obsessed about the possibility that my life might be over—or at least the one I wanted. Was I going to ever teach again, was I going to drive a cab for the rest of my life? I returned to New Mexico shortly after Labor Day to find out.

We hired a lawyer in Santa Fe named Mark Donatelli. He was a rugby player—he started the first rugby club in New Mexico—and he knew about me. We paid him a $10,000 retainer. The weird thing is that Mark drove a convertible and as he chauffeured me around town I got a little nervous. There were still a couple of locals in Santa Fe who very much wanted to kill me—G being one of them—and here I was being turned into a moving target by my lawyer.

Mark was able to get the district attorney to agree to a pre-prosecution resolution. That means the state would drop the charges if I continued to live crime-free. To help make that an easier decision, I had arrived with letters of recommendation from colleagues and superiors who discussed how I had cleaned myself up and turned my life around and was once again a positive force in society. I had to pass a drug test there, too. The agreement was that I would regularly submit to drug tests in New York.

The idea is that it's pointless to go to the expense of prosecuting someone who isn't dangerous and not likely to commit a crime again. Especially if that someone no longer lived in New Mexico and was thereby another jurisdiction's responsibility. That was me. The state of New Mexico apparently wasn't interested in me at all, because they didn't follow through on anything. I didn't hear from them again until I got my papers a couple of years later dismissing the charges—essentially blotting out my criminal record (well, at least until US Customs caught up with me).

After returning home to New York, I still had to deal with the bottomless bureaucracy that was the Board of Education in New York. New Mexico had freed me, but I spent hour after hour at the board headquarters on Court Street in Brooklyn talking to the board's private investigators to convince them I was worth the continued risk. Their concern was warranted—after all, I was teaching children—but it should have been fairly obvious by now that I was a man on a renewed mission.

They, too, finally relented and I returned to East Harlem, although this time as a gym teacher. The gym is where I ruled. The kids were tough, but I was tougher. At forty years old you're still pretty strong.

In some ways, I'm not sure how I was able to quit drugs cold turkey and work my way back to a successful life and career. I'm sort of dumbfounded by it.

I quit drugs a day at a time, without preaching a day at a time. I didn't go out and tell people, today I'm going to do X. The simple explanation is that I started living a little better. I started to realize that there's more to life, started feeling a little better physically and stronger mentally. My mother always told me that her side of the family had a very strong will. Maybe I inherited that.

There's a certain triumph at looking in the mirror in the morning and not saying, "Fuck, where's that next fix?" Rather, by saying: Today is going to be a good day. Let's try to get through today. Let's try to get a task completed. I didn't have time to sit back, since I was penniless when I arrived home. Being penniless will help straighten you out too. I had no economic resources. I remember those early times back in Long Beach when I was trying to scrape together a few dollars to just feed myself and Lara. I used to think, *holy shit, if I had just saved that hundred dollars I shot in my arm, if I had not spent the $60,000 of my* *retirement savings that I withdrew my last months in Santa Fe and infused it in my veins.* Heck, I could have made money in real estate. Invested. After all, New York was cheaper in the eighties.

The truth is that I didn't have time to score drugs anymore. I didn't have time to think about it, because I didn't have money and therefore I wasn't going out looking.

I just wanted to feel better about myself. And each day, very slowly, I started to feel better. I also had responsibilities. So it was a combination of trying to be a real parent, and trying to scrape together a living, that got me concentrated on staying clean. I'm not much of a meeting guy—but I don't want to discount meetings, because I did go to a few of them. But eventually I got into my own spirit, without the meetings.

I had also moved to Manhattan's East Side from Long Beach, again with Lara in tow. In those days, landlords wanted a letter from your bank attesting to the fact that you had some assets. This would have been difficult for me, since I had none. But a crazy thing happened. I went to talk to a banker and had a long chat with a guy, told him what I did, how I wanted to be part of the community, and he ultimately wrote a letter for me saying I had $10,000 in the bank. Even though there was no chance that any bank would so much as loan me a nickel at that point.

Letter in hand, I showed up at a 350-square foot, fifth-floor walkup in a classic New York tenement on East 73rd Street in the Yorkville section—what used to be Manhattan's German neighborhood. The rent was originally advertised at $599.99 a month, which was going to be a stretch for me. It was a circa-1890s railroad flat with the bathtub in the kitchen. But when I got there the landlord told me there was a mistake— the apartment was rent controlled at $299.99 a month. That was a steal at the time. My daughter Lara still lives there all these many years later.

A few months after moving in, King happened. At that time, the city had its own certification testing for teachers, which superseded New York State's requirements. This was handled by the Board of Examiners, which was a political patronage machine that has since been discarded. If you got on the Board of Examiners, you had a plum job that didn't require much in the way of work. But it was the system, so I took the exam for guidance and phys ed and passed them both. Having a license in guidance from the city gave me the opportunity to look around and interview for open positions.

That led me to King, where I got an interview with the assistant principal—with whom I would later have a titanic battle after she became principal. She was a phys ed person like me, and needed a guidance counselor, because they were firing some inept people. Immediately, my personality took over. In business parlance, I have great people skills, which basically means I can get along with most people and kids really like me. And I like them. Even our assistant principal liked me, at the time.

That's when she placed me as the counselor for the English as a Second Language (ESL) students. That's where it began. Kids from Haiti and Central America and Africa and me trying to figure out their needs and how they could be met. It could get a little rough. Sometimes the African American kids would get into beefs with the Haitian kids or the Central American kids and there would be fights. I would step in and work on bringing both sides together.

In the meantime, I was coaching at Manhattan Center for Science and Math. I was their first soccer coach. It was near my old job at PS 96. That's where I first started developing soccer players. In fact, I had these two Moroccan brothers who both ended up playing for Columbia University, a top program. One is now a cardiologist and the other a lawyer. I still see them. I coached there two years, taking that squad from nothing to making it into the second round of the playoffs.

Once I got transferred to King on the West Side I didn't want to have to travel back to the East Side to coach. So the athletic director of LaGuardia High School for the Arts found me and asked me to take over his soccer program, since the school hadn't won a game in years. Again, I built a little team, nothing great, but we turned them into a competitive team. That's when I was offered the job at King.

One thing that didn't change with the new job at King was my financial status: I was still dirt poor. Coaching didn't provide much more money, but I noticed that the lawyers' basketball league was using our gym every night so I got certified as a ref. I had already been a soccer and wrestling official but now I was refereeing basketball every night, even high school games, as well as volleyball. I was doing anything I could to make ends meet.

Working that many hours in the gym didn't leave time for a social life, not to mention romance. But then it happened. I was walking down the stairs to ref yet another game of basketball, and she was walking up. Two ships passing in the stairwell. Eyes met; smiles met; well met.

Connie and I are now together for more than twenty-five years. Of all the things that being at King would bring me, she was surely the greatest. But let me tell you how we started. Connie was there in her capacity as chief administrator of one of the law firms in the league. In fact, she had just joined Fischbein, one of the city's most politically connected firms, and some of the women there had taken her to dinner followed by some lawyerly spectating at the gym. Both of us knew we would see the other at some point in the future. There's a Yiddish word for it: *bashert*. Destiny.

Sure enough, a few weeks later, Connie appeared, as a volleyball player. I was there as a ref of course, and I made sure I was the one who called her game. Or as Connie tells it, "he waltzed in to ref my game and then threw the game our way." Whatever it took to get her attention—even some generous line calls—was not beyond me that evening.

Connie noticed, and in all likelihood so did the opposing team that was getting the short end of the whistle. But this wasn't the Olympics. After the game ended, the players left the court and Connie had made her way up the bleachers to a point where she was sitting by herself.

I looked up. She looked down. She tapped her hand a couple of times on the bleacher, telling me to come up and sit next to her. I bounded up there like a retriever bringing a duck back to its master. Down boy.

I am, as I mentioned, a talker. A people person. And Connie was a people I dearly wanted to talk to. Which proved easy to do. Within about fifteen minutes, she knew my entire history, nearly every last horrifying detail about it, including my precipitous fall from a responsible educator to lowlife addict.

You might think, well, a smart person would have said, "nice talking to you" and taken off. But Connie is a smart person. And we discovered we had a lot in common in our histories, both good and bad. She appreciated my honesty.

Like me, Connie is trained as a counselor. We had the Midwest in common, too. I went to school there; she grew up there, in Springfield, Illinois. And counseling is what she started out doing until she moved to New York with her then-husband. She soon realized two things: her marriage wasn't going to last, and she wasn't going back to the Midwest. That's how she got into professional management: she translated her human resources skills to managing the operations of large law firms.

We also shared a somewhat curious history of soccer and addiction. When Connie lived in Chicago, she was in a relationship with a soccer player who played in that city's European leagues. She knew the game and the passion that goes into it.

Sadly, she also knew the pernicious power of addiction, because her youngest brother had fallen to it. As she tells it: "my late brother was in some ways a clone of Martin. That's why the two of them kind of bonded. And he became very supportive." She wasn't scared off by my history. By the time I met her, I had been clean for years. She understood, and believed, that I was finished with drugs for good.

I was, however, just getting started again with soccer. And at the time Connie didn't know much about my coaching ambition. Like the rest of the administration, she thought I was a guidance counselor!

During our first couple of years together, Connie couldn't come to many of our games because she was working until 9 or 10 p.m. every night. That's just the demands of having that kind of job. But there were diversions, including trips to places like Washington D.C. where we would play against a local team and take in the sights. It was during those trips, which took place over the next few years of our relationship, that Connie got to know more about our kids. And we both got to know one of them especially well.

# CHAPTER 14

# Mansour

MORE THAN A THOUSAND YOUNG men have been part of MLK soccer under my watch. They want to live the American Dream, and I'm the nurturer and protector of that dream. You try to do the best to treat everyone equally, but you can't always. Because some kids are just special. And not necessarily because they're especially skilled, but they have some inner magnetic power that draws you toward them.

When I have met or heard from African parents who send their kids here to play for MLK, I have often heard the words, "He is your son now." Those are inspiring words and I try to live up to them. But for one very special player, that actually happened.

Mansour Ndiaye became our son.

Let me explain. Mansour's parents sent him here in 1997 to get an education. And did he ever. His is a familiar story. He was fifteen years old when he landed in the United States from Senegal, in West Africa. He spoke the language of his people, Wolof, and the language of the colonialists, French.

African parents care as deeply about their children as do American parents—that's why their kids are here in the US. But they can't play the same role, either because they have to remain in Africa or because the struggle to earn a living in New York City is so difficult for immigrants that they must expend enormous amounts of time working to make ends meet.

Mansour's parents sent him to live with an uncle who had already established a beachhead of sorts in the States. They wanted to give him an opportunity they never had, naturally. He arrived in June, a few months ahead of the school year. First job: learn English. By that September, his uncle felt he was fluent enough for school and the two went off to the Board of Education office to register him. They were told to retrieve his school records from Senegal and to make sure he had the proper vaccinations, which were obtained in due course.

They were simply looking for a decent high school, any school. Then the Board of Ed did something that would change our lives: instead of choosing a school in Harlem, where he lived at the time, they sent Mansour to Martin Luther King High School. Perhaps they knew that other Senegalese kids were there.

Little did I know, but I was about to hit the lottery. I would find a player who not only would lead us to championships in 1998 and 1999, but who remains part of our lives forever.

Mansour was sent in to see a guidance counselor, and in the sort of chitchat that takes place with a new student—what are your hobbies, what do you like to do when you're not in school—he mentioned that he loved to play soccer. He didn't think that it would be possible in New York City. Wait here a minute, the counselor said, and she left the room. Mansour wasn't sure where she was going or what she was doing.

A few minutes later she returned with another guidance counselor, me. Mansour says that I gave him sort of a funny look when he asked to join the team. He was a bit of a chunky kid but hey, he was Senegalese; he probably had decent skills, I figured. And I am all about giving kids chances. So I gave him a full rundown of the program, about how good our team was going to be that season. And I invited him to join the team, without ever having seen him play. Mansour jumped at the opportunity. He assumed that he would prove himself at practice.

But there were no practices scheduled before the next game. So when he showed up for the game, I gave him a uniform—and a seat on the bench. I wasn't going to risk playing him sight unseen. It wasn't until we were winning by a couple of goals, a comfortable margin, that I figured I could risk putting this rank newcomer out there.

Then the magic happened. He first made a clever run into an open space—a telltale of a good soccer brain. But the moment he touched the ball I knew we had someone special. When the ball was played into him, he trapped it and turned fluidly and then made a perfect pass to a teammate, who scored an easy tap-in goal. Brains, technique, and execution in one little cameo that couldn't have taken more than five or six seconds. It was all I needed to see. The next game, and for the rest of his high school career, Mansour was in the starting lineup. He would go on to become the captain of the team, its spokesman, French translator, and a leader in every way. The other kids looked up to him.

After the game, I did what I usually do, which is cease being a coach and turn into everyone's guardian and mentor. I make sure they have their subway and bus passes so they get home, make sure they know they can call me if they need anything. Make sure they have food. At one point, Mansour made one of those calls. He mentioned to me that he didn't have a bed, could I help him find something decent to sleep on? The next thing he knew, a new bed was being delivered. I couldn't have my star midfielder not getting proper rest—but it's something I would have done, and have done, for any of our kids. Kids like Mansour, who come to this country with very little support so they need someone to hold their hand and walk them through the systems.

When I later visited Senegal with Mansour, I learned that the community takes care of itself. Yes, you are somebody's son or daughter, but everyone in the community takes care of all the sons and daughters. It's true, as Hillary Clinton wrote, that it "takes a village" to raise a child. Over time, that creates a very strong bond between you and the people around you. That sort of defined Mansour's relationship with me and

Connie and my daughter Serene. We became an extended part of his community.

The Thanksgiving of his first year here, I invited Mansour and a couple of other players over for the traditional turkey dinner. Seems that he never left our family from that day on. As Connie puts it: "Mansour's the kid that never went home. He's just special. The first thing you noticed is that he always had his head in a book. He was serious about his studies and just a wonderful kid; you just loved him the second you met him." Mansour puts it this way: "I think the fact that I got to a point where I liked them, and they liked me—it was just natural." And so it was. One by one the other players took off to do whatever teenagers do, but Mansour stayed until he was the only one left. I had to put him in a cab so he didn't have to take the subway to 125th Street in Harlem, where he was living.

That didn't make me any less tough on Mansour as a player. All the players know that I am not shy about hollering at them. But they are left with no doubt as to where my heart is. As Mansour put it: "He's a very intense guy who really, really likes to win but wants nothing but the best for this players, his kids, his children." And he laughs when he thinks about me chasing him with my "crazy crystals" before games.

As obvious as Mansour's soccer skills were, his intelligence stood out, too. He and Connie are the family intellectuals, and they could talk for hours. Still do. That's one of the reasons our relationship became more special. It's just how things worked out. Mansour began spending more and more time with our family. His American family.

Mansour went to King before the years in which it became known as "horror high." He knew how to apply himself, graduating as salutatorian with a 94.5 average. That's an incredible achievement for someone who didn't speak English when he arrived here. And Mansour loved MLK because everyone loved him: peers, the faculty, the security people. He had a great experience. It was wonderful for me; I couldn't ask for any better.

We were thrilled when he put aside an opportunity to go pro to instead continue his education at the University of Connecticut. We took him there as proud parents, our African son who had made the grade to a Division I school. I'm sure the village was proud too. This was another new experience for him. We had to buy him the things that every college kid needs, such as sheets and towels.

His career at UConn was just as outstanding as at King. We tried to go to every UConn game we could. In his junior year, UConn would lose in the NCAA semifinals. But in his senior year, we flew down to North Carolina to watch him and his UConn teammates win the national college championship with a 2–0 victory over Creighton— almost as good as winning the city title!

There's no doubt in my mind—or his—that Mansour had pro talent. But his intellectual side won out. Instead of becoming a pro soccer player, he became an educator. He stayed on at UConn to get his masters and PhD and then joined the faculty. Pretty amazing.

Mansour now has a ten-year-old, who could tell you as much about Grandpa Jake and Grandma Connie as Mansour can. He comes every summer to stay with us near the ocean in Long Beach. Even though Mansour's parents are still living, they are happy to know that on this side of the Atlantic they have someone looking after their kid. And Mansour is lucky enough to have a spare pair of parents.

## How to Find Your Own Spirituality in Recovery

The one question always asked of me is: How did you do it? How did you get clean after all those years of abuse? How do you not relapse and stay clean?

I stopped using all drugs and alcohol decades ago, and through willpower and the grace of God I am still clean today. I remember all the sickness, despair, and hopelessness I felt when I did go

*(Continued on next page)*

back to the needle. That path was hardly straight. There's a saying that it's harder to "stay clean than to get clean." Man, did I live that. I relapsed so many times.

I was in treatment numerous times. I would go to the hospital in desperation—or to avoid jail—and check myself in. Failing so many attempts to stay clean made me depressed for my character flaws. Despair, disappointed, embarrassed—never caring about anything but my next fix. I was a disappointment to so many, but mostly to myself. All that was left of my self-esteem would be gone forever. Or so I thought.

The horror stories, many retold in this book—the drug store robbery, scoring at the housing projects, ducking a bullet blazing past my head, the numerous break-in capers with my junkie "friends" and on and on—make the case that I was living to score and scoring to live, if you could call that living. Getting through the day, getting that "fix" is all that matters.

Oddly, it's the same as getting clean. You need to get through the day, stay straight that one day at a time.

I remember driving my brown Subaru Forester, glancing out the window, and looking at all those normal people who were not junkies. Always asking myself what it would be like to just not use, just be a regular person like I used to be.

My horror story of addiction, maybe like so many others, continued for years. Will this ever end? Will I ever get clean? How do you spiral down so hard, so fast? How do you let your self-esteem get so low and how do you get out of that hopelessness of your addiction?

I was addicted to opiates for three years. I was busted for check kiting, forgery and fraud, and shoplifting. I was offered help, hospitalized/detoxed, and sent to a few treatment centers. All with no success. Finally, I lost everything I owned and resigned from my job as a counselor and coach. My life was in shambles, I hit bottom. Sometimes, this is what it takes.

My cleanliness evolved. You just do not wake up one day and say you're not using your drug or drugs of choice. My journey was different, yet just maybe not so different. Broke and without my spirit, losing my soul and with all of $1.23 in my pocket, I returned to New York from New Mexico. At a time of becoming homeless and penniless, I dropped to my knees and prayed for help.

That is where it all began to change. Prayer . . . and remembering that most prayer begins with the absence of God, you just keep praying.

My athletic ability and years of training probably helped me withstand the physical demands of getting straight. But I'm also a spiritual athlete, someone who learned to explore other beliefs, someone who learned to train his mind as well as his body.

My first journey to real understanding of the mind and the spirit that goes with it was my introduction to Silva Mind Control. Living in dreaded Detroit in the early seventies, working in the Downriver area near the toxic Detroit River, I met Steven and Cathy Storms. Steve was a teacher at the same school I'd worked at in Trenton, Michigan.

One day we got introduced to a program started by Jose Silva and a technique that allowed you to use your "bio computer" brain to your advantage and program in positive thoughts. Silva Mind Control teaches you to use your inner self, more than your cognitive self, to better yourself. A personal growth program. We got hooked, in a good way, into something beneficial. A mantra that Silva used: "Every day in every way, I get better and better."

This self-empowerment program was the beginning of something that brought me inner peace. There was something about it, a realization that we have so much power to heal, and to feel better all within ourselves.

*(Continued on next page)*

We took classes, Steve became a certified instructor, and for the first time ever I felt this inner power and a knowledge of using less of your brain and more of your "psychic" ability to program in positive thoughts. There is a Silva Method technique I used and actually still use more often than any other. One of the post-hypnotic suggestions you can give yourself is that when you hear a negative comment or a pessimistic point of view, you say "cancel, cancel" to yourself, and when you do, the negativity will have no influence over you. To me it was a kind of mental cloak of protection. This program methodology included positive thinking, visualization, meditation, and self-hypnosis. There were steps, lessons. Classes were fun. It was, briefly, a movement.

No matter what method or belief works for you, I recommend that you build your spiritual awareness. Become one with God. Muktananda, one of the many spiritual leaders I looked at along the way, professed that God dwells within us, as us. Spirituality can get you to become involved in your religion and yourself, allowing you to move from your fears and regrets. Spirituality can fit into your current framework of religion. Religion can be thought of as a set of beliefs, rituals, and practices regarding belief in God. Spirituality is a personal search for meaning in life, for connection with all things, and for the experience of a power beyond oneself.

Learning about your inner self is important in addiction recovery because addiction takes away our ability to see inside ourselves. Addiction keeps us from choosing anything but the object of our addiction. An addict's ability to grow and change is limited. Addiction takes over one's life. Although the life of an addict can seem random, chaotic, and uncertain, it is actually very predictable and extremely routine. Score, live, score, one day at a time. Life is solely about getting the drug, using the drug, and recovering from the drug, repeated over and over. Life becomes monotonous. Not being able to be our true selves stops us from growing. Spirituality is about growing and evolving.

Spirituality is recognizing a power greater than ourselves, which is grounded in love and compassion. It is a power that gives us perspective, meaning, and a purpose to our lives. It is a desire to connect with more than ourselves, to connect with everything. To fully recover from our addiction, we must reconnect to our inner self and our true spirit. We search for purpose in our life and connections beyond ourselves to grow and change. Change is our constant . . . we must keep evolving spiritually, emotionally, and physically.

Learn to be mindful. Mindfulness is the concept of living in the present, not worrying about the future, not stressing about the past, just living in the moment.

Support groups are also a key to moving forward in a clean world. I hung out at AA, and sometimes Narcotics Anonymous. Latching on to any words of hope and encouragement. You cannot do it alone, so do not isolate yourself while working to be clean. Support groups work.

# CHAPTER 15
# Outcast

I AM NOT A GOOD loser. I admit it. Another son of New York City who played that other kind of football, Vince Lombardi, was more than right when he said, "winning isn't everything, it's the only thing." I've felt the full validity of that statement in the last two decades, during which time our teams at MLK have won all but 20 games.

Being too successful, if that's possible, seems to engender a certain anger among sports fans. The great teams all have their haters because they win too damn much: the New York Yankees, the New England Patriots, Manchester United, Real Madrid. It's just a bit much when it's directed at teenagers. And it still happens to us today. We win so often because I somehow cheat—every year. Or at least that's what the haters say. Man, I must be really good at it. But instead what I'm really good at is making kids believe in themselves and their abilities.

I learned very early at King that not everyone would welcome my ability to turn a losing team into a powerhouse in a short period of time. We won our first championship in 1996, which was something of a surprise to the reigning powers such as Newtown and Canarsie. When we repeated in 1997, it became abundantly clear that King was now, true to its name, the new king of high school soccer in the city.

But we did not get the respect that our kids had earned. Instead, we got retribution and racism. In 1998, being good almost cost me my job—and exacted a terrible toll on two of our kids, who would be robbed of their futures through no fault of their own. Indeed, they were victims of a pernicious level of jealousy among coaches and parents that is still a sad part of high school sports. Even worse than the pettiness of rivals, they were also victimized by malevolent school administrators out to get me. Because we won too much. Because I took immigrants into our school and tried to help them lead decent lives and because people have no idea how difficult a life these kids have.

Henry Iwuchukwu was royalty. His father, Joel, was the chief of the Ibo tribe in Nigeria. He was one of seventeen children from Joel's two wives. The family was Christian and the chief disapproved of anything, especially soccer, that might distract Henry from Bible studies. So little Henry sneaked out of the house to play and rapidly developed into a budding starlet. He was nine before his father happened upon one of his games. Perhaps it was a message from God—this kid can play, chief—but Joel understood that Henry was gifted. So, the chief gifted him with new soccer shoes.

Bishop Dike hailed from Owerri, one of eight children of a fish-monger. Bishop didn't have to hide his ability, and by the time he reached his teens he was in Nigeria's national team system. So, too, was Henry: both were selected for the national under-17 team, which at the time was a pivotal step toward a professional career for an African player, because unlike today scouts then didn't visit Africa much.

The boys' dreams of being discovered seemed to get a boost when a Nigerian-born obstetrician, Obi Okehi, promoted a tournament in his hometown, Macon, Georgia, for the under-17 national teams of Brazil, the United States, Ghana, and Mexico. Nigeria would not send its national team, but Okehi, a licensed FIFA agent, sponsored a squad of twenty Nigerian youngsters, many of them national team members. Disorganized and ill-equipped, the team arrived late for the matches and soon found itself stranded in Macon, the expense money and return plane tickets having mysteriously disappeared.

Henry and Bishop were lost in America. They made their way to Atlanta, where they found food and shelter within the community of immigrant Nigerian cabdrivers, street peddlers, and food handlers. Then they hopped a New York–bound bus with a teammate, Chika Echendu, who had some contacts there. Specifically, Chika had a cousin and that cousin knew a Jamaican woman in the Rosedale section of Queens who agreed to put them up. Although they were bunking in Queens, the cousin also knew that the best soccer action—and the potential money—were a borough away in Brooklyn. That's where Ralph Bavaro came into play. Ralph was a fixture. He'd played some semipro in Italy but in Brooklyn he was better known as a coach.

Brooklyn has long teamed with ethnic talent. It had Italian, German, Polish, and Irish teams, but also Ukrainian, Hungarian, Bohemian, and even Swedish teams. Then came the Central and South American teams. Bavaro was delighted. He arranged for his old team, Napoli United, to play against their great rivals the Brooklyn Italians.

Weeks later, with the high school season ended and the club football season in full swing, one of my players, Kevin Isa, came into my office. He knew of two great players, and he encouraged me to come see them. He told me they were Nigerian and playing for Real Napoli. "You got to see these guys, Jake," Kevin insisted. "Best I have seen. And I don't think they're in school." Too good to be true. I was doubtful but I called Ralph, an old friend.

"Hey, Ralph."

"Jake."

"One of the kids tells me you've got a couple of Nigerian kids out there worth seeing."

"I have now," he said. "They could be gone tomorrow."

Club soccer in New York is like club soccer the world over. Money lubricates things. Your best player is always likely to be offered a little money to play for a bigger, richer club. I knew that if Ralph was this worried about his two Nigerians being poached, they must be good.

"Jake," he went on, "I need to get them into school. I need to get them something to keep them happy. These kids are lost."

We talked. He told me a little about the situation of Henry Iwuchukwu and Bishop Dike. They lived way out in Queens near Kennedy airport, which is about as far away from midtown as you can live and still be in New York City.

"These kids," Ralph said, "they're just sixteen and they can play. They need to be looked after. Will you meet them? Listen to their stories at least?"

Of course I would. I'd listened to many stories and I was constantly amazed by the journeys many of these kids had taken—the risks, the dangers, and ultimately the courage they needed to survive. And now they were sitting in my office. This seemed like the end of their adventure. We could offer stability and hope.

Henry and Bishop were as eager to please me as I was to please them. They had the tough exteriors of kids who had been through a lot, but they were still kids. I showed them pictures of our championship teams, newspaper clippings, and gave them t-shirts. I told them about the school, about the lessons. I could tell that they missed the structure. They were kids and they wanted somebody to look after them again. Sixteen years old was too young to be making one's way alone in the world's craziest city.

Perhaps I oversold them on the structure part. They were appalled by what they saw at their new school. Here they were two kids from a supposedly third-world country, but they had arrived when MLK was bottoming out, when the tabloids were proclaiming it Horror High because of violent crime and criminally bad administrators. As Henry would tell the *New York Times*: "There was no discipline. Back home they hit you with a stick for not paying attention, coming late, using bad language. I would never put my hands in my pockets when an older person talks to me." The corridors were a sea of gum-chewing, hollering, streetwise kids. There were gangs and there were cliques and there was more attitude than you would get at a hip-hop awards night.

Despite the culture shock and the language barrier, the two managed a B average from the getgo. They enrolled in after-school tutoring. Teachers complimented me and the boys on their work, on their manners, and on their readiness to engage in the classroom. Those early academic terms were proof of the boys' character. They wanted learning. They wanted the tools for assimilation. I got them a home, living with Cal Nwabudu, an assistant treasurer of Chase Manhattan Bank and president of the Nigeria United Soccer Club in Brooklyn.

That summer I took Henry and Bishop with me to Middlebury, Vermont, where a team of King players and alumni called the Harlem Jakes won a tournament. The players also won the hearts of the locals. They were perfect houseguests, whose respect for elders left a deep impression on the host community. At the same time, our kids had never seen such wealth. Bishop was the star of the tournament. And he was given a little piece of the fantasy weekend to take home with him. He so charmed his host family with his earnest need to succeed, they gave him a computer before he boarded the bus back to the city.

Bishop had an inner beauty to him, a pure essence. He was like the Pied Piper—little kids would just follow him. He loved it. He would kick them the ball, make them laugh, pick them up. My youngest daughter, Ana, was seven years old at the time. After a game, she'd run to Bishop and he'd lift her onto his shoulders and walk around the park with her high in the air.

Henry and Bishop were on their way to the big-time stage. Henry would control the center of midfield, spraying passes around like a quarterback with ballet skills. Bishop would run and run up front, his skill and power taking him past defenders for crucial goals every time he played. Henry and Bishop thought they were living their dream, on the path to becoming soccer stars. At an Adidas-sponsored soccer camp, they made the all-star team and were listed as preseason high school all-America predictions.

That 1998 season, with Bishop up front and Henry at midfield, was the best at King to date—and we had not lost a game in the previous two seasons! On the field, King was untouchable; we ran the table on our way to a third title, bringing our win streak to 53 games. Bishop and Henry were not the only Africans on our team. Our defensive-midfielder, Macky Diop, was a tall lanky kid from Mali with an amicable personality and gifted feet. He would later star at St. Lawrence University and go on for a master's degree. His countryman, Garan Diarra, was as mean on the pitch as Macky was amicable. He would take people's legs off. An assassin. Of course, I loved him. Another St. Lawrence grad.

We were even deeper in keepers with Bouna Coundoul and Ronnie Lowe of Trinidad, who was the smaller of the two but incredibly agile. Talk about good hands, he played steel drums on weekends, not for fun, but to make enough money to survive. We had a South American star for good measure. That was an Ecuadorian midfielder named Edison Brito, who was just five feet, seven inches, but he could vault defenders for headballs and run forever. The word was out. MLK had something special.

As we neared our 50th consecutive win, the King story began to resonate. One of our big-city tabloids, the *Daily News*, started covering us regularly, as if we were one of the local pro teams. The Madison Square Garden Network devoted a special to us. This was heady stuff, indeed, and brought about a darker response—far darker than I could have ever imagined, for both me and the kids.

The 50th game proved to be a bad auger. We were playing Humanities High School and, due to injuries, I had only 12 players available. At that point in my career, I didn't have enough resources to maintain a large roster like I do today. We went down to 11 available, as someone had let me know that our keeper, Ronnie Lowe, had missed too many days of school and was therefore not eligible. His grandmother had died and the loss was particularly tough for him, because he lived at her home. As her illness worsened, he had missed a couple of days in school to be with her. Too many. So I pulled Ronnie from the lineup after a few minutes.

Brito had an issue, too. Student athletes must take a physical and obtain a parental consent form. I lacked the parental consent form, although Edison was eighteen, old enough to provide his own consent form. Because of his family difficulties, I had let the matter rest. But a monitor from the PSAL, who was somehow made aware of this, made me drop him from the team. This is a kid who was working weekends at a bodega, trying to make enough to stay in school and keep his soccer dream alive. His dream denied by the bureaucracy, he left school to stock shelves in Macy's. Before long, Ronnie dropped out too. The waste of talent was obscene.

So on this day against Humanities, we struggled to get a full team on the field. We won 7–0 anyway. MSG Network and the *Daily News* were there to document it.

Beating Humanities was easy; we simply had too much talent for them. But beating the political hacks and their flunkies was an entirely different game. And we were up against cheats, none worse than the aforementioned PSAL monitor who had been fired from his job as a principal. Why he was allowed near students is still a mystery to me, but he scrounged a job at the PSAL and decided that he was going to be the bad cop of soccer. He was going to start looking into the program, because if we're winning, we must have been doing something wrong. Right? This was the problem of being a dynasty: you got treated to institutional backlash.

Sure enough, Hunter College High School sent a tape to the PSAL. It's a game Hunter played against us before the playoffs, and Edison was in the lineup that day. Hunter College! I should have known. (By the way, this Hunter was not related to the Manhattan Hunter Science High School in my building. It was an elite, mostly white school starting in elementary school and going through high school, with helicopter parents never far away.) When we played the year before, these highly educated parents started hurling abuse at my kids. "Go back to Africa!" they screamed. "You kids don't belong here!"

Understand, this is liberal New York City. The score was 10–0 when this started up. I don't deliberately try to run the score up, but any team should be allowed to play up to their skills. I shouted back that they were a disgrace. I told the ref. I reported it to any official I could— my principal, their coach, and their principal. Nobody seemed to care.

Now, a year later, they had sent a tape with evidence of Brito playing against them. Obviously, they'd been tipped off about Edison's position. These parents wanted both games, each won handily by us, forfeited. More than that, they wanted both victories to count toward Hunter's record. Even worse, the parents insisted that King should be banned for the entire season for cheating.

At this stage, officials went back through our games to a match against Stuyvesant. At that point, they decided that we must forfeit the Stuyvesant game as well. So two big, white, rich, elite schools got forfeits off us because one of our kids lost his grandmother and didn't follow protocol.

Any thoughts that this would go away would be quickly dispelled. My trials with the school administrators, including the school principal, were just beginning.

A meeting, to which I was not invited, was held between a PSAL member and our school principal and I was told it involved a tape of the ineligible Brito playing. I was not provided any comment or explanation. Due process had been left on the bench.

Finally, my principal asked me about the forfeit. *Screw it*, I decided. If that was how important the kids were to them I'd take the forfeit, and lose the winning streak, and then go ahead and win the title anyway. If there's anyone to blame, let it be me. We needed to move on for the kids and for the school.

Moving on came in the form of a disciplinary hearing, to which I was invited. Our principal was sitting behind a desk with a couple of union representatives. They're supposed to represent me. The season was almost at an end. The Hunter parents were still raving and making racist attacks on our players. These people were well-connected—whereas, in contrast, half of our kids had no parents here— and they were trying to get our players kicked out of the playoffs so their mediocre children could have a trophy. Yet ultimately, the school suspended me for the alleged crime of "egregiously sloppy paperwork." Thomas Liese, the Board of Ed's lawyer, backed up the decision with these words in the *New York Times*: "We're not going to say he hasn't done good things for kids but we are going to say that it wasn't enough to offset some unfortunate errors." So apparently having an exemplary graduation rate and turning out honorable young men didn't cut it when it came to filling out paperwork.

Meanwhile at King, rapes, assault, and attempted murders were taking place, teachers were consorting with kids, and teachers were consorting with teachers. The situation had me seething.

Thankfully, the union reps stepped up to the plate, insisting that I be guaranteed my coaching job the following year. Paperwork was signed, agreeing that I would be reinstated as soon as the playoffs were over. In the meantime, I would be gone. Pronto.

With the playoffs on the doorstep, a very good friend of mine, Glenis Pole, was appointed interim coach. Fortunately, Glenis, the nicest guy in the world, knew what had to be done.

Playoff time is always stressful for me. Yet during my suspension, when I felt like a pariah, banned from being with the kids (although, technically, I remained in touch with them as a guidance counselor at the school), the stress ate at me. My health deteriorated, and I developed colitis. "I've been shot and stabbed scoring drugs," I told the *New York Times*. "Detox was hell, but nothing in my life has been as bad as this suspension." That was no exaggeration.

Of course, I saw the boys, who practiced in the gym every evening at the same time. They would exit the side door on 66th Street and I would meet them at 66th and Amsterdam. The kids would huddle around me and hug me and start chanting, *Jake! Jake! Jake!*

We also had several meetings. They were comic book clandestine, but they put my future on the line. Discovery would risk my reinstatement, and it would finish the boys' season. We'd meet at Burger King after school. I'd cover my head with a hooded sweatshirt. We got burgers and huddled around to discuss strategy and life. We'd all hold up newspapers so that we appeared to be reading intently. From behind the papers the discussion of team tactics and practice sessions could be heard. We posted lookouts at the front and back doors, behind mailboxes and streetlights on the corners.

I'd give a little talk, about getting focused and winning the playoffs. I told them this is life—sometimes, really lousy things happen that you can't control. These are the things we have to face, but we are a team. Everyone is going to be okay. They knew that I wouldn't be with them on the sidelines, but I would be with them every step of the way. Somehow.

Kids are kids. They need reassurance. They needed to know I was doing well. They needed the praise and encouragement. They needed to be told they'd done nothing wrong.

During this time I was constantly talking to Glen about naming the starting team. As the playoffs progressed, I would sit in the stands and have a runner sprinting up and down to Coach Pole telling him who to sub. The first two rounds were at River Bank Park where I couldn't be banned because it is a state park and I'm a taxpaying New York resident. I ran my runners quite blatantly. People were watching. I didn't care. There was a part of the sixties rebel still inside me. And after all, I was once an armed desperado in New Mexico. This was, in a good way, child's play.

The whole situation stalled the team's progress. Long Island City failed to show for our scheduled first-round encounter and the game had to be played two days later. We won easily, 4–0, but LIC protested that King had not submitted a roster before the game. Fortunately, the protest was thrown out. But can you imagine forfeiting a game because of a missing signature?

Our next opponent showed the continuing beauty of the city's melting pot: we met and defeated a team of Poles, Ukrainians, and Russians from Madison HS in Brooklyn. That moved us on to the semifinal round against another Brooklyn school, Wingate. The match was set at Downing Stadium on Randall's Island, the now gone but hallowed ground in the shadow of the Triborough Bridge where the Brazilian legend Pelé and the New York Cosmos had made their NASL debut a few decades earlier. True to the city's diversity, Wingate's ethnic mix included a lot of talented Trinidadians and Jamaicans. Perhaps ironically, their coach had been quoted saying it wasn't fair that we had players from Africa. Huh? Perhaps he wasn't aware how many Africans were taken to the Islands as slaves several centuries ago. Despite Wingate's ample talent, we cruised 3–0.

Now, the final. Roosevelt, a rising team from the Bronx that had come through the other side of the bracket and was a surprise finalist, would be our opponent.

I'd already decided I wouldn't send messages down for this one. The kids knew what to do by this point. I decided just to scream out instructions as blatantly as possible. You can't stop a guy from screaming from the stands. A few good friends—Paul Gardiner, the well-known soccer writer; Arnie Ramirez, the coach of Long Island University; and Pat Begley, a friend who two weeks earlier had given me a gift of a book on Scott of the Antarctic, so that I would understand the challenges of life—decided to sit around me for solidarity. So there we all sat, up in the bleachers. I got the sense that Roosevelt High's principal and one of her teachers were trying to intimidate me by sitting nearby as if to say *you don't dare try to send messages down to the field*.

Henry Iwuchukwu scored the first goal 28 minutes and 54 seconds into the match. "We love our new coach, but we still want our old coach back," he told the *Times* after the game. "He's like a father. He was there in spirit. He told us that he would be. That's what won the championship." Then Bishop put his stamp on the game and the season. He took a ball from 30 yards out and curled it into the top corner of the net. It's a ridiculous piece of skill.

The second half belonged to Bishop. He was really banged up with all the double and triple coverages he'd been getting. He had to leave the field at one point to get a bandage over a slash cut on his knee; he also needed to replace a dressing on a five-stitch wound on his chin from getting smashed in the semifinals. He uncorked a 25-yard screwball into the upper ninety to make it 2–0. And then another. All over. Roosevelt never even threatened. We won 5–0. Day of days. A beautiful win.

And then a beautiful moment. When the game was over the kids on the pitch unfurled a banner. *Jake We Love You.* I treasure that banner to this day. The kids chanted my name as they went out to collect their trophy. All the way to their bus, you could hear it like a war cry. My heart felt light for the first time in weeks. I was still not supposed to have any contact with the kids, but I waited and gave them all hugs as they exited the stadium.

This game, it turned out though, was far from over. As soon as I was done and the bus departed, I saw Joan Burroughs, our athletic director, coming over to me. "Jake. They're lodging a protest. They say Henry and Bishop are too old. Frank Brown, Roosevelt's coach, is running around telling people the boys are 'not teenagers.'" I was bewildered, though not surprised by the protest. They seemed to come in hand with every big victory. "Nothing will happen, "I told Joan. "They're not too old." She's not done, telling me: "Oh yeah, and another thing they're protesting about is your coaching from the stands."

"Fuck them all," I say. "It'll go away."

Wouldn't it?

Sure enough, there were complaints to the PSAL right after the game about me shouting from the stand. By that point, I was so weary it scarcely mattered.

The media brought one small break in the clouds. Bob Lipsyte of the *New York Times* wrote a column that sided with my position. So did Gardiner in *Soccer America.* They knew this wasn't just about soccer. It's about getting the kids a better life. They could see the big picture.

The articles hit the system at the right time. Peg Harrington, the Deputy Chancellor for the Board of Education, read what these guys had to say and took steps to make things right. Letters calling for my reinstatement began pouring in.

And so it was that I was summoned to a meeting along with my union rep and the AD, Burroughs. I was again given written notice that my suspension was temporary, and that I would be reinstated:

*It is agreed, effective at the conclusion of the Fall 1998 soccer season, the grievant suspension will be rescinded. Although receiving an unsatisfactory rating, it will not negatively impact upon his ability to apply for, and receive the position of coach for the 1999–2000 school year . . .*

I was still filled with worry. I'd pushed the Bishop and Henry matter to the back of my mind. I knew the truth. I knew how old they were. I knew they were legal. What was the worst that could happen?

By Thanksgiving, PSAL soccer commissioner Mike Turo was diving into charges that Bishop and Henry weren't legit. Roosevelt people were all over the papers now, making false accusations about the boys. At the *Daily News,* a paper that traditionally had the back of immigrant communities, especially Irish, Italians, and Jews, one reporter went fully nativist, repeating accusations without appearing to ask salient questions or to give a damn about Bishop and Henry.

Turo's people came into the school. Initially, they ruled the boys eligible. They then went back and decided to interview the boys without any adult present to help them. They refused to allow me to attend. The boys were interviewed separately and alone.

The claim was that the two boys had used eight semesters of athletic eligibility in Nigeria before arriving in New York in 1997. They just kept repeating that they had never graduated high school, which happened to be true. School officials refused to let me have anything to do with the process. I couldn't represent or counsel the kids, and I was refused the right to get the boys' parents involved from Nigeria.

The boys' records, which the PSAL had already approved the previous year, were sent to an "African expert" in the school system. The expert decided that the boys graduated. There was no academic transcript, just a piece of paper saying they took these courses in 1996. I kept saying to them that these are meaningless testimonials, not academic transcripts. Nothing mattered though.

Henry and Bishop were declared to have been ineligible. In this tragedy and miscarriage of justice, I was told that I would not actually be reinstated at the end of the season. The records were never fully investigated, and nobody went looking for academic transcripts that would provide the boys' results in various grade exams in Nigeria.

The atmosphere turned caustic. Not long afterwards, forty of New York City's nearly 120 boys high school soccer coaches signed a petition to rescind Martin Luther King's 1998 PSAL soccer championship. They wanted the title that we had won fairly to be declared vacant. They wanted the banner and trophy held at MLK to be returned and for the MLK nameplate to be removed from the trophy. In an unprecedented move, they requested that all players on future MLK rosters be verified independently regarding meeting current eligibility requirements.

All those requests were denied. The PSAL, like most soccer leagues in fact, has a sensible rule about "warehousing" protests until the end of the season. If you have a protest to make, you make it at the first opportunity, not after your team has been eliminated so you can mail in a protest along with your sour grapes. Our title was left intact but our reputation, and mine, was in tatters.

Among the players, Henry and Bishop took the developments most to heart. Proud, honorable kids, they were suddenly seeing their names in print next to words like "cheat" and "liar." Everywhere the boys went they heard talk of what was going on. A couple of blameless kids get caught up in a noxious situation not of their own making. Maybe they're doubting me, too, because I couldn't seem to stop the attacks. First they had been abandoned in the US and left adrift. Having found a life raft at King, they were now being branded as cheats by a cabal of losing coaches.

Bishop and Henry began to drift away from King and the trouble it was bringing them. They started cutting classes. They looked to make more money from soccer in the short term and began playing with the bigger, more moneyed Brooklyn Italians. The boys would pick up cash on the indoor circuits and play weekends with the Italians. Bishop and Henry were still living with Cal, but suddenly Cal was struggling with them. He wanted them to stay at King. He found them some work, but soccer agents were tugging at the boys' sleeves, whispering about the big deals ahead of them.

One day in December, Henry and Bishop sat down in my office, their faces filled with gravity. The more voluble Henry, taking the lead as usual, told me about how embarrassed they were about these articles in the paper. "Nothing is true," he said quietly and firmly. Then Henry announced they were going to quit school.

I begged them to tough it out.

I lost. The dream of being professional soccer players was still alive and was still realistic for Henry and Bishop. We had plans for the boys to go to college, then still the path to the professional ranks and Major League Soccer. I was making contacts. MLS was growing, and I was friendly with a few development guys. Options were blossoming. Bishop and Henry seemed destined for greatness.

"We were ashamed," Henry said. "We see our names in the papers, not for scoring goals, but for being called liars and cheats. It goes deep in your spirit when people look at you as if you did something wrong."

On and on, the same argument. How do you explain that newspapers don't take these things into consideration? Two kids. How they feel. How they know it looks. I could see the shame and hurt on their faces. They'd been framed as cheats and frauds. Seventeen-year-old kids. Not arms smugglers. Not cheats. Not criminals. Their crime was their talent.

For a while, I lost contact with them. I was fighting for my own existence as well my own integrity. I feel guilty about that period in their lives. I wasn't there for them. My soul was ripped. I was devastated by the suspension. I was accused of cheating.

And then more shocking news: I knew I had hepatitis C, a payback of sorts from my days of drug addiction. A biopsy indicated Stage II liver disease, which means you have to go on drugs (the irony of which does not escape me) or face a liver transplant. My doctor was begging me to start Interferon treatments since I had neglected my condition to a dangerous point. Now my strength was waning. I went into a depression. I lost thirty pounds in two weeks.

Meanwhile, Henry and Bishop were receding, two teenage planets drifting out of my orbit. No more school. Within a few weeks they were being watched by Dynamo Kiev, the biggest club in Ukraine, which liked what they saw. Dynamo Kiev pursued their interest and invited them to Europe—a move on the path to full-time contracts. The deal was room and board now and a contract later. Bishop and Henry were afraid to leave the country in case it all went south and they couldn't come back. They decided against Kiev.

The boys sought a new direction, even from each other. They left Cal's home and went their separate ways. I tried to get them to engage in a degree equivalency program, to no avail. Instead Bishop made his way to Philadelphia where, I found out, he has a brother named Ibian. To support himself he became a street vendor, peddling watches. Henry eventually landed in Philly too before splitting for North Carolina.

Back in MLK I wasn't doing all that much better. In the spring, I filed a grievance against the principal for refusing to reinstate me. Like the boys, I'm a man without a country. Never mind the trophies, the commendations, all the wins, and all the kids that I had helped. I received a U rating at the end of the school year—as in unfit.

But I was not without advocates. In fact, a knight rode to my defense in the form of Joan Burroughs, MLK's athletic director. She understood what a raw deal I was getting and she, like me, was concerned about the welfare of the kids. Her friendship and support got me pumped up to fight this one out.

I suggested to her that we start our rescue mission at the Nigerian consulate and ask for help. The consulate was across town on the East Side, near the United Nations building, appropriately enough, and we went together on a cold winter day. After passing through security we were escorted upstairs and started to meet embassy personnel. First, there's the Protocol official, who listened patiently enough to our tale. We were then directed to the educational representative, who handled counseling and transcript evaluation for Nigerian kids who want to go to a US college.

We were worried that two New York City teachers would be shuttled around for a couple of hours before being shown the door, but this man greeted us with warmth. He listened to the saga of Henry and Bishop and gave us the number of a man who would help—Stanley Ogunedo.

Stanley had a diplomatic mien, a short man who was precise and eloquent. He was, in fact, a former consulate official turned book merchant and president of the Africana Legacy Press, a publishing house. That might explain the oversized briefcase he hauled around with him. More importantly, he knew his way about the educational system in Nigeria.

Stanley and I met in a coffee shop near the consulate a few days later. "We will do this Jake," he assured me. "I know how to do this. The boys have been wronged."

I tried to conjure up some optimism and asked him about the next step.

"I'll need an airplane ticket," he said.

Finally, some hope. This whole experience had felt like a bad acid flashback, comparable even to my hopeless existence as a heroin addict, when desolation was constant. In recovery, there's an acronym, HALT. It stands for hungry, angry, lonely, and tired. That's what withdrawal is like, and I was experiencing the same thing now. Except that I was not missing the negative existence of heroin—I was missing the passion of coaching. I tried to keep in mind another saying from my recovery period: your worst day clean is better than your best day on dope. I kept reminding myself of that. Stay positive. Stanley was a sincere and forceful presence. That helped, too. He was positive, and I fed off of that.

But first and foremost, we needed to get Stanley to Africa. A friend of mine, Roy Khan, came through. I met Roy when I coached his fourteen-year-old son in the US Youth Games over the summer. Roy was from Guyana—a doctor who became a huge fan of our program. He knew what the deal was for kids like Bishop and Henry. When I told him the whole story he offered money to help cover Stanley's plane ticket. I came up with the rest needed for Stanley's expenses and he and I shook on the deal. Game on.

Stanley also had a life of his own, of course, and a business to run. He couldn't get the free time to travel for months. He ultimately reached Nigeria to discover that the school system had gone on strike. There was no choice but to wait it out. Back in the city, the wheels of the school bureaucracy were grinding slowly, as they always did. While Stanley was trekking through Nigeria from one region to another to gather papers for Henry and for Bishop, my case against the Board of Ed was trundling ahead.

And the stakes were getting bigger. After a number of hearings, we had reached what's known as the level three grievance stage—the final step before arbitration. The Board of Ed informed my union rep, Tom Dromgoole, that it would try to have me terminated. The board's rep kindly offered me a year's suspension instead of termination.

At this very time I was taking Interferon to treat my Hep C. Interferon is horrible, a cancer drug with a host of side effects, none of them good. Maybe, though, feeling this badly would have another side effect: I decided to go all in. I was not going to accept a suspension when I knew Stanley was hunting for the documents that would exonerate me and prove that Henry and Bishop weren't cheats. I refused to lose.

Except that we did lose. The grievance board ruled for the Board of Ed. My head was now on the line in an arbitration showdown. The case was scheduled for September, just as the team was beginning to play again. Every day that summer I tried to do something to bolster my case. And to bolster my own wellness. And I waited for Stanley.

My story was now fairly well known, and perhaps it didn't hurt that MLK is just a couple of blocks away from the CBS News broadcast center. We caught the attention of *60 Minutes*, which decided to cover our story. From there the board suddenly went into stall mode, seemingly trying to delay the process as much as possible. They probably figured that if they could delay the case beyond the soccer season, the heat would dissipate. But that played into my hand too. We needed Stanley to get back with the goods. It's a chess game, and I was the one with the most to lose. The *60 Minutes* team interviewed a number of my players, including Bouna Coundoul, who told them that I helped make him an American: "We are the tree; but Jake is the roots. If they cut him, we all are going to die. So Jake protects us, gives us what we need, advises us, and helps with our education. Without him, we do not know what to do."

Of course, *60 Minutes* dutifully found someone with the opposite lens: Howard Ranzer, the coach of Newtown, whose team we'd beaten for the championship, called me unethical. He repeated the allegations against Bishop and Henry. "He played men against boys," Ranzer said.

The first hearing took place in mid-September at the Arbitration Court in Brooklyn, in this astonishing room where the people in other non-criminal disputes wage their own arbitrations. The arbitrator was an ex-judge who very much looked the part. The Department of Education ended up delaying the process further, persuading the judge to move the case to October. They were succeeding in pushing a resolution almost past the soccer season.

But they didn't plan on Stanley returning from Africa, with the goods. He delivered them at the grimy Port Authority Bus Terminal on 42nd Street—the very spot in which the boys first set foot when they arrived into the city. We sat in a busy coffee shop as he handed me the documents, as if I had picked them off the menu: school transcripts, official records, test results, and academic histories, each containing the original stamped proof of authentication. His summary: "From the documents, it appears the boys only completed JSS 3, which would be equivalent of the 9th grade in the United States." Signed: Stanley Ogunedo.

The confusion, and controversy, had its source in a set of spurious documents sold to the boys by a Nigerian con man when they were stranded in Georgia. He said the papers would enable them to enroll in any high school in the country.

Stanley brought the truth back to America. His investigation had been as thorough as that of any police detective's, and all above board: he was able to secure parental permissions to retrieve the documents.

Faced with unassailable evidence, the Board of Education quickly folded. What choice did it have as opposed to the base accusations that had been leveled at me? I was reinstated immediately, on October 7, 1999, after an eleven-month suspension.

Two days after my reinstatement, our principal was reassigned to a job at the Department of Education's central office. The Chancellor brought in Rudy Crew to turn the school system around.

"It's vindication for me," I told the *Times*. "But it can't make up for the pain and suffering of four wonderful student-athletes, all of whom dropped out of school without their high school degrees. I'd like to win a fourth title this year, but more important I'd like to make sure they all get back on the tracks of their education."

It was already too late for Henry. Lacking a green card and a school or job that could sponsor him for one, he was deported.

I at least had to find Bishop. So I went to Philadelphia with Robert Lipsyte of the *Times*, who had covered us for years. Bob had taken interest in Bishop, whom he called "the sweet, freckle-faced African dreamer."

Philly has undergone a renaissance since 2000, but in 1999 there was still a lot of urban decay to navigate. And we were in the middle of it, a desolate run of vacant lots and abandoned buildings called the Badlands—the South Bronx on the Schuylkill. We knew from his brother that he was working in some convenience store and we eventually found him, standing behind a filthy window of bulletproof plastic.

Here's how Lipsyte reported it:

*"Now, I'm outraged," he shouted at a moldy wall. "How does it happen that the best striker in the country comes to this? Is this what America does to people who come here to make something of themselves? Who did this to him?"*

I know of course who did this to him. The coaches like Ranzer who had called him a cheat. The administrators who couldn't bother to put in the effort to discover the truth. Bishop and his brother earned $4 an hour at the C-store. He was wasting his life and he knew it. "I am sorry. I missed a lot. I should be in college," he said to me.

I wasn't there to chastise him for his judgment. I wanted to find a way for him to succeed. I told him it's still possible that I could get him with the right coach. He returned to New York with us that evening. He later promised to return to school, at least to earn his G.E.D.

There was no happy ending. Bishop couldn't keep his commitment to earn his G.E.D. and wandered back to Philly, working the same shitty jobs to try to make a life out of it. Gradually, he grew mature enough on his own to realize that he was wasting his talent. He began working out with the Temple University soccer team and working on that G.E.D. He was moving toward his green card.

And his soccer career began to spark. He had been badgering Gus Skoufis, part owner of the Westchester Flames, to give him a roster spot. Gus knew he was good enough, but Bishop needed $200 a game to make a go of it. So Gus invited Bishop to try out with the Flames, hoping to keep him interested until a roster spot opened up. Twenty minutes into a scrimmage game in a New Rochelle park, Bishop collapsed. CPR was performed. The rescue squad arrived in ten minutes. An autopsy showed a defective heart valve. Bishop had never had a comprehensive physical exam in his life.

I will never forget that sweet kid, one of the major losses of my life and career. And I will never forgive the mistreatment by the grownups who were supposed to help him. From my standpoint, if Bishop and Henry had not been driven out of school by racists and jealous opponents, they would have likely advanced to be scholarship students at a university. And it's just possible that Bishop might have gotten the medical exam that would have discovered a damaged heart. No exam would have been needed to show that Bishop exemplified "King heart."

And he was part of a team that was just beginning to show how good it was. We would not lose a game for the next two years, a run of 39 games and two more city championships.

# CHAPTER 16

# A Program, Not a Team

LET ME EXPLAIN MY ROSTER: it can accommodate forty players. Last year we carried six goalkeepers, which is at least three more than any team would need. A lot of coaches would say that's insane. But we can count on two volunteer goalkeeping coaches to keep these kids inspired. There is no junior varsity, there are no freshman teams in New York. There's no funding for them, so they say. In essence we are running a soccer school. Not like it's the famous La Masia in Barcelona, but we take charge of the lives of forty kids. Oh yeah, and we do so without a field.

The way the kids get here is evolving. The growth of American soccer has given rise to very sophisticated youth programs. Here in New York we have organizations such as Manhattan Soccer, Downtown United Soccer, and Central Brooklyn soccer all running elite programs. So, youth coaches will call me and say, "I have a kid I'd like you to see," meaning that they're special enough to play for King, and the coach wants to further the player's soccer education. And then I meet the kid and sometimes the parents, if they're here, and tell them about our program.

Many of my team members now come from these clubs. Coaches I know recommend them and they apply to a school in the building that best suits their educational goals and needs. There are players whose brothers, cousins, and even fathers played for me. Coaches through-out the city recommend kids to come to King. The downside is that we now have lost kids to the academy programs run by professional teams like the New York Red Bulls and New York City Football Club. These teams demand a fulltime commitment from players. They won't let them play for their high school teams, which I think is a shame. They'll tell these kids that they can be pros, but the truth is that 99 percent of them won't be. And worse, the clubs will cut them just as quickly as they find a better kid to replace them. It's brutal.

One of the most important things in our structure is that we have a coaching staff versus a single coach trying to manage forty teenagers. If there were only one coach we'd have a team, not a program. When you get other coaches involved, including volunteers, we're more than just a team. I've been absolutely blessed to be able to team up with some incredible educators and coaches.

Associate head coach Josh Sherron is the taskmaster of our first team. Josh is a former pro whom I met through a Nike connection. He remembers that at his first MLK practice as a volunteer coach, in 2006, a couple of the kids started brawling and he waded in to sort it out. Some people might have seen chaos, but he saw opportunity and need. I don't think he's ever missed a practice.

Interestingly, Josh had had other professional plans before his arrival at King. He was going to become an entrepreneur, until des-tiny intervened on MLK's behalf. Josh is a New Jersey native who was studying business at Seton Hall University in the gold rush days before the Great Recession. He'd even come up with a good business idea and was in discussions with several venture capitalists for funding. Or, as he puts it: "We were all going to get crazy rich by creating a soccer social network: connecting the underground soccer scene."

Instead, the economy would collapse, perhaps one of the best things that could have happened to King soccer in the sense that it put Josh at a crossroads: start again down the path of entrepreneurialism or take a vow of poverty, of sorts, to stay involved in high school soccer. He chose the kids. He became so devoted to our students that he decided to become a teacher himself. He's earned two master's degrees in education and teaches English literature to 10th and 11th graders at the Urban Assembly high school. He was going to be an Internet wonk, but King has changed his life. And he has in turn changed the lives of so many our kids. Josh is like me, a man on a mission. "Teaching is the hardest thing I've ever had to do," he says. "It's the world's most difficult job."

That job can be made more difficult by a culture when kids absorb parts of our culture that sometimes look down on education. There's a certain pride in hip-hop culture, for instance, of rejecting education that can infect our students. Our soccer kids are struggling all the time to advance themselves, to grow and learn, and they can be surrounded by a toxic culture of peers who think it's cool to not do smart things or tear down people who try to do smart things, or to achieve. In other schools, athletes are the heroes, the achievers. Josh tells the story of running into David Diosa, another of our former players who made it to the pros. David played before Josh arrived and had won several championships. "I guess you were the kings of the campus," Josh remarked to him. No, David told him, it doesn't work that way around here. That's why I'm so glad Josh is on the faculty to fight against that pernicious attitude against knowledge.

Good coaches collect good people and aren't threatened by their talents. I happened into Mickey Cohen one day in 2000 in Riverside Park. Mickey was a soccer lifer, in his mid-fifties then, and regularly came to the park with a soccer ball and a routine he would go through to keep in shape. Mickey had run into a well-known soccer referee named Felix Fuchsman, who told him that he had to see the kids from MLK play.

So Mickey made a point to stop by and watch our practice. He told me that he had observed in amazement as a couple of our kids warmed up at a nearby volleyball court by playing volleyball with their feet. "The ball never touched the ground," he told me. "I had to find out who these kids were."

And I had to find out who the guy was who was talking to my kids. I found out then that he was one of the best goalkeepers this country has ever produced. Mickey played at Long Island University under Dr. Joe Machnik, the soccer Hall of Famer and famed goalkeeping coach and now better known as a rules analyst and TV commentator. Later, Mickey would be trained by Hubert Vogelsinger, perhaps the best goalkeeping coach in the world at the time. It's as though Mickey has two PhDs in goalkeeping.

And what a career. He'd started in the 1966 NCAA final—LIU was a powerhouse then—and would embark on a remarkable professional career from there. In the 1970s, he played in the old North American Soccer League (NASL) for the Boston Minutemen, among others. He played in the Major Indoor Soccer League (MISL) with the New York Arrows, owned by his friend and fellow keeper Shep Messing. He played for the Hartford Hellion in that same league.

Even better, I would later discover that Mickey started his post-soccer career as a teacher and coach at Boys High for ten years before going into the family signage business. When we met, he was out of that business and coaching at the exclusive Dalton School, where New York's wealthy send their overprivileged children. No wonder he hated it. Mickey is strictly working-class Queens. That day it was pouring, but Mickey started working our goalkeepers out. He must have pounded balls at them for an hour. There was no question that this guy knew what he was doing. So I asked him, "Why don't you coach with me?"

When Mickey began pinging balls at Bouna Coundoul, he marveled that the young man between the sticks was an unpolished diamond. And Mickey and I helped him become one of the best players ever to come out of MLK. Mickey asked him directly, because that's who he is: "Bouna, do you really want to become a pro?" And when Bouna said yes and promised to dedicate himself to the task, Mickey told him flat out, "Then I will make you a pro." Suffice to say that Mickey is a no-bullshit guy and delivered on his promise. When Mickey gets together with him at one of our events, Bouna will say:

"You see this guy here. He's the first one who made me believe in myself." Which is pretty cool for a coach, the ultimate accolade.

And a couple of great things happened because of that chance encounter. I later convinced Mickey, who was a little down-and-out when we first met, to get back into teaching. Which he did. I still tease him about it, telling him that I saved his butt. But the fact that Mickey would go on to teach and coach another decade meant that more kids, athletes, and non-athletes would benefit from being around him.

When Mickey left in 2010 to take a position at Monroe College, guess who became our goalkeeper coach: Bouna Coundoul. And after Mickey retired from Monroe, I begged him to come back to MLK for 2018. Though I really didn't have to beg. He loves the game and the kids, so it was easy. Fortunately for us, our high school team could count on two world-class goalkeepers for coaching. I doubt there's a pro team in America that could make such a claim.

The great thing is that our players are now in the position of giving back, of helping other kids along the path they traveled when they were teenagers lost in America.

Bouna is one such man. He knows all about winning and losing. During his junior year, we had one of those heartbreaking 1–0 losses, to our hated rival, Newtown, in the final in 1999. Bouna promised me then and there that he would win the title back the next year. He made good on his word, allowing only five goals in 22 games and named All-City Player of the Year by New York's *Newsday*.

He's a role model for our players in that he went on to play Division I college soccer (Albany State) and then became a professional. After college, Bouna became a starter for his hometown New York Red Bulls and later played in Europe, in South Africa, and for the Senegalese national team as their captain. His skill was such that when games got tense, the clock was winding down, and you needed a big save from your keeper, it became known as "Bouna Time."

"Bouna Time Academy" is the name of the goalkeeping school he runs in the US. He's also coaching at Monroe College and the

Manhattan Soccer Club. And speaking of giving back, he opened an academy in his native Senegal to which I was delighted to donate apparel and training gear.

His path here is by now a familiar one. Bouna arrived in 1997 from Senegal, brought by his father to get an education and "get on my own path." The first Senegalese he ran into went to King and told him about me. It didn't take long before Bouna and his older brother came to meet me in my office. One thing was immediately clear: he had the size needed to play the nets. He was already six feet, two inches and had the hands of someone much bigger. I took him down to the gym and started pinging balls at him. Those hands clamped onto my shots, despite the fact that I could still shoot like a striker in those days. This kid was a keeper all right, in every sense of the word. I had no idea, of course, of what a great person he would become.

There was one problem though. I already had an excellent keeper, one of my "Trinnies," Ronnie Lowe. I told Bouna he was not going to be my No. 1 keeper. At least not yet. "The first thing that happened is that we got into an argument," he laughs now about our first few days together. He screamed at me: "You can't teach me anything!" Before long, Bouna would be in the nets.

It was probably not quite a coincidence that Bouna found me. In the first couple of years at King, I would journey all over the city watching kids play soccer—to Van Cortlandt Park in the Bronx, where you can find Africans, Albanians, and Irishmen; the Metropolitan Oval in Maspeth Queens, where the old German-American league began play in 1923; to Alley Pond Park and Flushing Meadow Park in Queens, near Citi Field where the Colombian and other Hispanic communities would hang out; to Randall's Island, which sits between the Bronx, Manhattan, and Queens and is the ultimate melting pot.

Show me a pickup game and I can pick the most talented player in about thity seconds. Spotting talent is one of *my* talents. I'd find kids like Bouna playing pickup and tell them that they could play for a first-class team at King if they're interested. In the pre–social media days,

I'd give out my business card to anyone I thought might connect me with soccer talent: taxi drivers, supermarket clerks, doormen, people wearing soccer gear.

The word got out. Way out. A few years after Bouna arrived, a woman named Aissetou Ndiaye Lo came into my office to talk about her son, Mohamed, who was a great ball player, she assured me. She told me she had heard my name, and who I was, at one of the markets in Dakar—which is the capital of Senegal. That's how far the word had traveled about King and Coach Jake. And now she was here with her son, looking for an opportunity. The only problem was that the kid, who was about 6-foot-5, was a basketball player. Had he been a keeper like Bouna, well, maybe we had something. No, he was more of a power forward, but I was able to steer them into the hands of our basketball staff. He went on to play for a Division I basketball program.

Bouna will tell you how he and his teammates got through some of the rougher times at MLK. They would gather in my office at lunchtime to talk about school, soccer, and life. They represented kids from all over the world, and all over New York, trying to keep their dreams afloat in a sea of trouble. He later told me that I was the glue that held us together. It didn't matter to kids like Bouna that he was from Senegal or that someone else was from Jamaica, that they were from different cultures and religions or that their English wasn't great—they all had the common language of soccer to bring them together.

They fed off of one another, even if they were competing for playing time. When you have forty kids on a roster, it means twenty-nine of them won't start. It means most of them won't even play in the game. But the kids on our roster have always been quite ecstatic and honored to be on the team. The young ones in particular, because they know they're going to have to wait their turn—we tell them that. Prepare them. And you prepare them for disappointment—because life is full of disappointment—but if we do our jobs, they're not all that disappointed.

As I mentioned previously, I could never do my job alone though. I think the soccer gods were looking out for me when they sent Kimani

Calnek to MLK. Kimani has lived a multicultural, multisport, multinational life that he is now putting to service at King as a parent coordinator at the Urban Assembly Media School as well as his role as director of youth development for soccer. Sort of multitasking. He works with our youngest kids, a bear of a man with the touch of cub.

Kimani grew up on Manhattan's Lower East side but attended the United Nations School. Later, his parents moved to Westchester, where he could claim that Pelé's daughter was his babysitter. Even better, he spent a lot of time in Brazil, where his mother was pursuing a PhD. "That's where I caught fire with soccer," he says. As a teenager, he also became fascinated with Japan and would spend summers there, learning Japanese. Now that's worldly. And he's known what it's like to live in a different world, a different culture, like many of our players.

Kimani was recruited to play soccer at Claremont College in California, but decided to focus on academics his freshman year. Then, he says, he made "one of the worst decisions of my life" and played American football for a year, during which "I never touched the ball." So he switched to yet another sport, rugby, and touched the ball a lot, winning a national championship in the process. His coaching blueprint, though, came from another sport, basketball: his father was an AAU hoops coach and pro scout who later started a basketball development program in Jamaica that got kids into American high schools or college scholarships.

Kimani got his start by volunteering with a soccer club in the South Bronx: after his first season he was so impressive that they hired him to run the youth program. That's when he began seeing the same things that I had for so many years: kids from Africa and even the Middle East with great potential and potentially greater problems. In his words, "we were doing a lot that stuff: immigration services, social workers, help with housing—the laundry list of things that these kids go through. They think it's going to be golden roads and they realize, 'wait a minute I've got to live in the Bronx? This is like Fallujah.'"

Kimani found out soon enough about King and directed some players our way. But once Josh and I finally met with him, we discovered that Kimani was a great fit at King. He may think of me as some crazy grandpa at times—he calls me Trump's good twin—but we are very much operating at the same wavelength. It turns out we even have the same birthday.

It's Kimani's kind of leadership that keeps the kids focused, excited, and game-ready. Even for those on the bench, the kids all celebrate each and every victory. It's an ecstatic feeling when they see the championship, whether they're on the field or not. The good part about being good is that we get a lot of kids into games because we win four, five, six nothing or more. Even in a lot of the early-round playoff games we will win, scoring quickly, and I'll put in these young kids. I'll put the younger kids in as long as they can maintain our competitiveness—and against most teams they can. You'll never know how good they are unless you put them into the game.

More importantly, you just prepare them to be part of the King family, to have King heart. To embrace being part of something bigger because you're part of something special. You made the team. You got your uniform. You're part of King Soccer. You're doing something to be proud of for the school. You're wearing that King jersey. That King team warmup. You look good. You just stay warm on that bench with your other teammates, stay together.

And they get trained. The thing is, because of the coaches who help me, the kids get daily training, more so than they would at any club. We really train them the same way we train our varsity. The players feel that too: some of them asked to go to trials for the New York Red Bulls development team—part of Major Soccer League's program to have academy teams at every franchise. When they returned, they told us: our team is way better, and so is the intensity of the training. They're not part of a bigger system at MLK. They are the core of what we do.

The thing about coaching inner-city soccer is you don't have a lot of parents who get involved. And that's not because the parents don't care. They do. The problem is that inner-city soccer has parents that have to work, and have to be at work when their kids are playing. Some of them will never get a chance to see their kids play. That's really heartbreaking. On occasion I will hear, "Why is my son not getting more playing time?" But very rarely do I encounter that because I'm not in the schools where helicopter parents can leave the office pretty much at will and then demand playing time for their kid and threaten to sue you if he doesn't get it. They care, too—just a little too much.

Our program is sought after because we win by sticking to our principles. I've been accused in some quarters of running a recruiting program. Interesting. Why should it be illegal for kids to choose what they want? And I feel I'm going to do my damnedest to give a kid a program and a benefit. That I'm going make sure he studies, he comes to school, that he's given the right guidance counselors, that he's on track to graduate. I hold our kids in a high regard and with a motto that playing soccer for MLK is about getting a better life.

That's what a parent wants to hear. A lot of these people have to struggle to make a living, to survive. And they just want to know that when they send their sons to school, they're safe. And I can tell them, "I'm gonna watch after your sons and if there's an academic issue, I'll find out." And I do. I'm in contact with every single principal and every single guidance counselor and when things arise I have to handle it. I really do, it's insane sometimes.

We are really strong about our King family. And in our family you do the right thing and you live by certain standards and morals, and be the right person. I cover areas ranging from sexual harassment to tardiness in school, getting to class on time, and studying and working really hard in every aspect of their lives. I really do. I've gotten more intense and more involved in that over the years.

That's why we have parents who say, especially among the African kids or the Island boys, which is interesting, "He's yours now. This is your son."

I have so many such sons by now. I ran into one of them recently. It had all begun with a call from a coach I know: "I got this kid," that's how it always starts. And he told me, "this kid got kicked out of the US national team camp. So I want you to go help him." Okay. He did not play well, he got kicked out. Nothing terrible about that. The kid was fourteen or fifteen. But it wasn't just about playing. So I call the mom, I get ahold of him, I bring him in. It seems that he's involved in gangs in Brooklyn, and that he's been suspended from high school and that he's not allowed back. They don't want him back in because he's a danger.

And so I said to the mom, "Well, why don't we try to get a safety transfer up to King? Do me a favor, send him to summer school, get his credits up enough to play, and let's bring him up so I can work with him." And so we initiated it, they initiated it because it's called a police report safety transfer. So it was that this particular student played for me. And don't get me wrong, he was not one of my easier players. But he was amongst his friends, he made King his family. He hung out with my Island boys. He fit in with them. He ended up graduating, winning a few city championships—and losing one because he was still prone to ridiculous behavior from the time to time. But that's not the point. I can forgive him because he didn't quit.

He still, to this day, loves me. And his mother loves me. I know that, as she's never stopped thanking me. He went off to play for Monroe College, which is a local junior college, and even started there. He played two years and afterward he was offered a full scholarship in Manhattan College, another great local school. And he played two more years. Now he's a college graduate and he's got a job, but he's also coaching at Manhattan Soccer Club. That's a better life than the life of a gang banger who ends up in jail.

Such incidents aren't isolated, though. In fact, something similar happened again this year. All of a sudden I got a call from Erol Phillips, a former coach from a team called the Rovers out of Brooklyn. He said, "Hey, I got this kid, he has troubles. Can you help him? Can you come and meet him?" I met the family. I met the dad, who's a night watchman. He looked concerned. The boy failed in 9th grade, but he passed barely in 10th grade, so he could play for me. And he was in a school in Rochester in upstate New York. They had to move him hundreds of miles outside of the city, he got in so much trouble. And yet he's made the starting lineup for me. He's now in line, more or less. More or less.

These are things that as coaches we try to work through and work out, so that we can have cohesiveness. Because of what we teach and I teach about King heart and King family. But even brothers fight with brothers.

Some of my assistants want me to take a more tough-love approach, but I have what I call a softfulness (for lack of a better word) for some of these kids, knowing where they came from. Coach Josh sometimes shakes his head at what I'll do. He'll tell you that time and time again over the years I take kids who are dysfunctional and just won't quit on them. In retrospect, there were some guys that I should have cut loose—those who hurt the reputation of the program. They used the team to be disrespectful. We've grown, though. And as our level of play has gotten higher, we've been less willing to tolerate those guys who don't even try to help themselves, or reject the help we offer.

Don't get me wrong; push me, it's over. Betray me, go play for the academy team, quit the team without telling me? Don't try to keep your uniform. I will ban you from school until I get my uniform back. Not because you quit; because you just disappeared. You don't just disappear. You communicate.

But when a kid's on the team and has some personality dysfunctions or is working through certain things, my counseling background kicks in. I just try to be a counselor who will be assertive if it's necessary. But also to have the compassion to understand and change. You don't find that in a tactical manual or playbook. Maybe that's why kids come here. And I'm so proud of those kids who fight through those troubles, whether it's an external environmental situation or a struggle with their own teenage psyche.

In one case there was a kid who was suspended several times for various offenses. At one point I had to beg him to go to classes. The coaching staff really didn't need this, and I had every right to write him off. But my persistence paid off eventually. As often happens, kids start to wake up and grow up and realize the consequences of their actions. Ultimately, in this case, the student saved himself with our help. At the end of junior year, he said to me, "Jake I want to be the captain next season." So, he went from a kid with a long disciplinary record to a leader.

Then there are kids who just take a little longer to bloom. One year, this was relevant to the last kid to make the roster. But I just saw a little sparkle, a little gleam that told me to be a little more patient. We were right at the end of the tryouts and I said to our coaches, I think this kid's got something. He was raw, a pure street player. Our job was to develop him into a team player. We found him a club team to play on, and put him under the tutelage of a terrific coach. Looking back, it's clear to me that this kid was a hidden treasure who just kept getting better.

That's just one of the reasons I am so reluctant to give up on kids. And I'm not alone in that. As I've said, every summer I'll get a call from a coach somewhere in the city, and the conversation always starts the same way: "I got this kid."

What they don't have to say is that the kid needs help in some way or another that they can't provide. Or they're worn out trying. Yet it's a kid they still think deserves a chance, an opportunity to thrive. And they know that I'm one of the few coaches in the system who's willing to take that chance on kids who are, for whatever reason, questionable. Or troubled. Or just a pain in the ass. Look, given what I've done, who am I to be too judgmental?

Yeah, we've been burned more than once. There are some kids you will never quite get through to. You can see it in the documentary *Coach Jake*, which covered our 2014 season. Two star players from two different cultures who for some reason tuned out to do their own thing. I can understand that, even if I don't like what it does to team chemistry. That's not the worst thing that can happen. Every now and then there are kids who leave the safety of the team to fall for the appalling allure of being a gang banger. It absolutely pains me, but at least we can say we've given it our all.

I always say you have to get into the heart of a kid—always showing the kids you care about them. No matter who the kid is on my team, I take a special interest and I make sure I talk to everyone because that's who I am. In return, I expect them to perform at an optimal level and respect my decisions.

We've saved hundreds of kids. We've saved kids who were homeless and keeping it a secret, who then went on to go to college and get a real job. We hear from them: "You guys saved my life." And in turn it just snowballs: we've done that for so many. This is an immigrant city and an immigrant country and today we have people come to us who are hard-working, humble, smart, remarkable human beings who are treated like second-class people. And we protect them to help them thrive. We've always done that work.

We're a little different that way. I run a year-round program. I make sure the kids are okay. For example, I might see a kid who shows up on a brutal winter day wearing two or three sweatshirts. Most people wouldn't think anything of it. But that sets off an alarm bell with me. It tells me that his family is so poor that he doesn't own a winter coat. That is not acceptable to me, and I make it my mission to go find him one. We run Friday night futsal during the winter to keep the kids engaged—and inside. We run a free summer program. I mean, no other school in the city does that and not many in the country.

So this so-called recruiting that I allegedly do is not all about signing the exquisitely trained, well-adjusted kids, inserting them into the starting lineup, and starting the video camera. It's about getting kids prepared for life. It's about taking risks on some kids, because God knows many of them have taken enormous risks just to get here. They've more than earned a chance.

## The Spirit Coach

As a coach, if you don't wake up happy that you're alive, the kids will catch on. They'll know you're an empty vessel, a blowhard. And because of my previous addiction, of being down and out, broke, because of everything I experienced, every day to me is a gift. So you've gotta approach every day as a gift.

I have heart problems and the other night, I felt my heart beating a little harder and I thought, *Hope I'm not getting another fibrillation.* It went up a little, but not to a level that was abnormal. I had to take my blood pressure and I had to take my pulse and I'm going, "Oh, shit. I don't feel right." And some days I just don't feel right. And then I say, "Okay, God. Come on. Let's calm this one down." And then, waking up in the morning is a gift.

One of the greatest gifts I've enjoyed is hiking, with my poles, boots, and all the gear. I love the National Parks and Forests. Places like Sedona, Arizona, and all over the southwest in New Mexico, Utah, Colorado, and Nevada. My hiking travels have taken me to Argentina and Iceland. I like it as much as I do the hustle of New York City. In general, it's about getting away into a peacefulness. Coaches can't be just focused on one thing in life. Don't get me wrong, I absolutely believe in what I try to preach to the kids. Family first. School. And then soccer. In that order. Sure, sometimes I put the preference on soccer because when the playoffs roll around every year, it's time to get to business.

I have a little mantle that serves as a kind of altar. I am sort of pan religious, pan spiritual. Hey, why limit yourself to a single deity, especially after what I've been through?! That's why I have lots of spiritual items, including my crystals, which I bring out for the playoffs. I have a whole repertoire of mementos for the play-offs, a spiritual all-star team. I have stuff from Japanese priests. I have a record-keeper crystal that I found forty years ago in New

*(Continued on next page)*

Mexico that I hold in my hand when the game's going on, or in my pocket. And I have a Buddhist bell that a Japanese monk once gave me during a trip to Japan. I've been in Italy and I went to the priests in the monasteries and said, "Will you pray for my team?" In Senegal, I've given money to marabous—you would call them witch doctors. They then sacrifice lambs and goats for their people, and the marabou feeds it to the poor. Then they sit around and they pray and some kind of writing goes on. Finally, I get this prayer token. I still got a bunch of 'em. And they go in my little spirit pouch.

There are very powerful souls on this earth; that I believe. Will it equate to winning every championship? No. But I'm a believer. I'm a believer that there is a spirit. There is a higher power. That's why I have met with African shamans in New York. (Hey, you can find anything here.) That's why my pouch is a spiritual grab bag: Buddhists, Muslims, Catholics, Jews, and shamans and ancient crystals from whatever spirit world they came from. I'm born Jewish but I'm sure as hell not leaving anybody out or anything to chance.

In all my years I've never felt that anybody on our teams worried about what religion anybody else was. In games, it's not unusual to see the Hispanic kids making the sign of the cross. When the African kids arrived they added their own outward signs of faith. I'll never forget my first introduction to Islam. We went on a trip years ago, in 1997, to Washington D.C. and the Muslim kids at one point stopped for the afternoon prayer. They just stopped. They faced the East. Got down. Laid down their shirts and just did their prayers.

What does this have to do with coaching, with soccer? The point of all this is that I get the kids to buy into believing that they have power (though I have to be careful not to push any or all school religions, which is against school policy). And then that extra little push gives us that extra little spiritual power that we need to win. I'm a believer. I mean, does God love soccer like I do? I don't know. Maybe he or she does. But I really believe in this stuff. I get into it a little more and more.

So it's great to have other desires in life—it could be marathon running because you love what you feel like when you're running. It takes you away from everything. Gets you in the state of bliss. For me, that takes the form of hiking in the mountains. When I hear the sound of nothing. The absolute sound of silence.

All too often, we get tied up in the mundane parts of life. And that includes coaching. But we always forget there's something a little deeper in life and I think that something needs to be explained or explored or talked about. Without a spiritual base we have nothing.

Trust me, after the life I led I'm covering all the spiritual bases.

# Epilogue

WHY WIN?

Our 2018 team was our best team ever. Not only that, as Mickey Cohen, our goalkeeping coach, put it, this was the "funnest" season he's had. According to Mickey: "Even with the great players we've had in the past, this team was special. When you have fifteen or sixteen kids that each have the ability and talent to take a ball, and apply a high-level skill and improvise—it would have taken an act of God for this team to lose."

And that stems from the fact that we did lose. Twice. We were defeated in the semifinal in 2014 and in the quarterfinals in 2015. Back to back. Heartache to heartache. For Josh and me, especially, those losses were crushing. A day after that 2015 loss, a group of players came to the office. They were devastated, too. Some of their teammates had been arrogant; they had assumed that, because they were King players, they could just show up and win the game. One year was a fluke, so they just dismissed it. Two in a row would be impossible, so they thought. Some of them even partied the night before, I would hear.

But as coaches, we know that anything can happen in a big game. The US beating the Russians in ice hockey in the semifinals at the 1980 Olympics? Impossible. The Russians had crushed the Americans something like 10–2 in an exhibition game right before the Olympics.

But they did not crush our belief, and the US turned belief into energy. We had belief at King and turned it into arrogance. Now these juniors were here because they couldn't bear the idea of losing another title. Never mind the fact that they had won 95 percent of their games. That wasn't good enough.

They told us: We want to go out with a championship. We can't leave MLK being labeled the class that never won. And they did. They worked so hard that we became a machine, that's how badly the boys wanted to win. We rallied together and that next season, 2016, we fought back to claim a massive double overtime, sudden death victory. Those kids weren't going to be denied a championship. They were so inspired to work hard to execute the tactics we devised for them.

Winning is what keeps me alive. In the 2017 season, I didn't quite realize we would be as good as we were. We just kept getting better and better. I remember adjusting our practices to include more complexity, which demands a lot more skill. The winning combination was the fact that we had a lot of talent to go along with the work ethic. Losing in the championship rounds in 2015 and 2016, in a way, made those kids a lot more mature. That was one of the smoother years I had, as far as personalities, as far as kids being responsible and responsive.

Ultimately, we won our games by large margins that year. The closest game was the final, which we won 3–0. We were winning other playoff games 9–1. We got hot when we needed to get hot. We trained nonstop on shooting because we weren't scoring enough in the last three weeks of the season and we were able to really put it together.

During the playoffs, I get excited and sickly nervous, as in not-good-for-heart nervous. My wife Connie knows to steer clear of me. It's horrible. My blood pressure rises tremendously, so I have to be careful. For example, even watching the World Cup I would take my pulse just to see if it was rising. My pulse is usually 40 to 60, which is really good. It goes up to 70, maybe 80, and then I get worried. So this is what happened during the season. I can't sleep the night before a playoff game. I wake up at four in the morning. I ask God to please let me have some sleep.

I've been doing this for four decades, and because of my insane desire to win there's now more pressure. We're never supposed to lose. There are 156 high school soccer teams in New York City, and MLK should never lose. It's self-imposed pressure more than anything, because at this point of life—after 18 championships, 480 wins, and a 97 win percentage—all that matters to me is winning the next championship.

I don't know why: I love the feeling that winning gives you. It just never gets old. Winning is everything; I almost hate to say it, but winning is everything. I don't believe it's how you play the game. Because if you play the game correctly you are going to win. That's the way I look at it.

At King, we don't discuss losing. Our kids are not prepared to lose, and they don't think they are ever going to lose. I don't anticipate losing, so I think they emulate me. They feel what I feel.

But lose or win, I've never stopped caring about the kids. I made sure they got on their way.

I've also emphasized the importance of being the best human you can be—which means teamwork and which means caring about your teammates. I remember listening to University of Connecticut Coach Geno Auriemma, who has won 11 NCAA women's basketball championships. The only thing he recruits is character. I instill that in them, that character.

It's for these reasons, I think, that I get so many kids who want to just make the team—kids who want to try out and be part of something special. That's why I keep as many as I can. It's the love of the game, the love of your teammates, the love of King soccer. Above all, it's King Heart.

# Afterword

## By Kyle Martino
## NBC Sports analyst

I FEEL LUCKY TO HAVE come across coaches during my career capable of making a lasting impression on me. Whether it was at the recreational or professional level, I was exposed to a few whistle-wielding wisemen who knew improvement goes far deeper than x's and o's.

Coach Jake encapsulates what makes a coach special. Winning is nowhere close to the teacher that losing is and for much of his life, Jake couldn't find a "win." Rather than let his misfortune and mistakes defeat him, he found the courage to overcome. His personal triumph now fuels a remarkable capacity to see the amazing potential in those fighting great odds.

I too found wins elusive at one stage in my life.

In 2009 I suffered a career-ending injury at the age of twenty-eight. A series of bad-luck incidents and a worn-out body brought an end to a dream I had since I was a child. I wasn't aware at the time, but that moment was the first time in my life I battled with depression. It's impossible to explain the dark, windowless room of depression to someone who hasn't felt the confinement of its walls. The fog I was living in felt endless and too thick to navigate. At that delicate inflection point in my life, I was showing self-destructive behavior that worried those closest to me. Through their support I found my way back to solid footing and immersed once again in the colorful glow of the beautiful game.

Like Coach Jake, I found strength and support through the game I thought I lost. I saw it not only as a way back to a healthy and fulfilling life for myself, but a way to connect with others looking to find love and support. It never occurred to me, coming from an affluent background, that soccer is a social enterprise vehicle. Many fighting great odds and ugly discrimination realize their true potential off the field based on what happens between the lines. At this point in our history, people fear learning about those who don't look, sound, or think like them, and soccer is one of the last bastions of shared experience capable of bringing those walls down.

Jake is proof that second chances work. His life demonstrates the pivot we all can make, and the incredible impact it has on those we come across. He did the work to save his life and now uses it to save others.